To Gayle

With Love

Sang C. Lee

The
WANDERER
나그네

by Sang-Chul Lee
and Erich Weingartner

Wood Lake Books
Inc

Photographs supplied by Sang-Chul Lee, except as follows:
front cover and page 123, Ron Cole/United Church Observer
page 81, Jim Taylor

Co-author Erich Weingartner was himself a refugee as a child, escaping from the communist advance in Yugoslavia to Austria. He studied philosophy and theology in Canada. In addition to being a freelance writer and photographer, he has worked for the Lutheran World Federation in Geneva, the International Documentation Centre in Rome, and the World Council of Churches in Geneva, where he was most recently Executive Secretary of the WCC's Commission of the Churches on International Affairs. His previous works include *Church Within Socialism*, a reference work on religion in Eastern Europe; *Human Rights is more than Human Rights*, co-authored with his wife Marilyn; and *Behind the Mask: Human Rights in Asia and Latin America*. At present he lives in North Bay, Ontario, where his wife teaches nursing science.

Canadian Cataloging in Publication Data
Lee, Sang-Chul, 1924-
The Wanderer

ISBN 0-919599-86-9
1. Lee, Sang-Chul, 1924-   2. United
Church of Canada - Clergy - Biography.
3. Clergy - Canada - Biography. 4. Korea -
Biography. I. Weingartner, Erich. II. Title.
BX9883.L43A3 1989   287'.92'0924 C89-091235-1

Third Printing 1990

Published by
Wood Lake Books Inc.,
Box 700, Winfield, BC, Canada, V0H 2C0

Printed in Canada by
Friesen Printers
Altona, MB R0G 0B0

Table of contents

Introduction

After I was elected moderator of The United Church of Canada, at the church's 32nd General Council in Victoria, B.C., several publishers asked me about writing my authobiography. I told them, and Council, that I had no plans to write a book.

When I returned to Toronto, a letter from Erich Weingartner was waiting for me. He said: "I think it is urgent you write a book about yourself as quickly as possible." Then he added: "You may be overwhelmed by work, so I want to offer my services as ghostwriter."

I accepted his offer, because Erich has been my friend for many years. He knows who I am. He shared my struggles over the years in the human rights movement.

He had already initiated contact with Wood Lake Books. Erich began a series of interviews with me. Shortly after, he began sending me drafts of the manuscript. I realized that Erich is an excellent writer. He produced a readable book from our talks. In fact, after reading it over, I felt his portrayal of me was perhaps kinder than I might have written myself. I say this with humility and gratitude. The stories in the book are mine; the writing skill is Erich's.

I did not realize that Jim Taylor was involved in this project until later. Jim is also an old friend. He and his wife Joan were present at one of my first meals in Canada, at the home of his parents, Dr. and Mrs. William Taylor of Union College in Vancouver, B.C., where I had come to study.

The writing of this book has reminded me of the love of my parents, brothers, sisters, and especially my late father-in-law, Dr. Kim Chai-Choon. I dedicate this book to them.

Sang C. L.

Introduction

I first met Dr. Lee Sang-Chul while working for the World Council of Churches in Geneva. My responsibilities as executive secretary of the WCC's International Affairs Commission included dealing with human rights abuses in South Korea in the late 1970s and early 1980s. Dr. Lee was a prominent and respected member of a worldwide network of church leaders engaged in this struggle.

His positive outlook and gentle good humor belied the often-painful inner conflicts which have marked Lee Sang-Chul's life. This I came to know only through the interviews I conducted with him in preparation for this book. Journeying with him through his past awakened powerful emotions in me. At times, the mere act of writing down his story moved me to tears. Perhaps this is because I too have been a refugee, a wanderer and an immigrant.

Writing another person's life story is an awesome responsibility. I thank Dr. Lee for his trust in allowing me to shape and systematize his words, though I have minimal acquaintance with Korean culture and no knowledge of the language. Whatever errors or misundertsantings may arise from this text result from that unfamiliarity on my part.

My appreciation goes to Jim Taylor for a superb editing job, to my wife Marilyn for tolerating my moods when the deadline nears, to my daughter Miranda for her critical reading of difficult sections, and to my parents for their prayers and encouragement.

Erich Weingärtner

The wanderer

As I fastened my seat belt in preparation for take-off, my heart sank. Suddenly I had a feeling I was making a terrible mistake. Why had I agreed to leave Korea, to fly halfway around the world to become a stranger in Canada?

I was going to Canada on a scholarship for graduate studies in Vancouver. My original plan had been to leave the year before, in 1960. But then came the student revolution in Korea, a bad time for a student pastor to desert his flock.

Perhaps I was beginning to panic because I had already moved too often in my life, each time under stress. As my wife and three daughters gave me farewell embraces at the air terminal, a heaviness descended upon me. Leaving them behind awakened powerful emotions.

My entire family history had been one of rootlessness. My grandfather fled with his family from Korea to Siberia. My father fled with us from Siberia to China. Then I fled alone from China to Korea. Since then, I had never seen my parents, sisters and brothers again. Was I about to repeat that history yet another time?

"Don't be silly," I said to myself. "Two years of study in Canada, that's all. Then you will be back with a S.T.M. degree and better opportunities to provide for your wife and daughters."

The plane sped down the bumpy runway. I felt its wheels lift off the ground, separating me from Korean soil. As the city lights receded into the night beneath me, the plane banked into a turn. Outside the window, a bright, translucent moon came into view. I recalled the brilliance of the moon in the mountains of Siberia, in the plains of China, on the road south with the Korean war close behind me. Would the moon look the same in Canada? Would my wife and I be able to watch the same moon at the same time, providing us with a tenuous link across the ocean?

As the plane settled into its cruising altitude, taking me ever farther eastward away from my homeland, my mind wandered backwards over my life. I remembered how clear was the night of our wedding. Then the emotion of that wedding day flooded over me, and I could no longer hold back the tears.

I cried at my own wedding. I don't mean merely a watering of the eyes, or the occasional tear trickling down the cheeks. I mean sustained, uncontrollable sobs, which my wife later told me lasted longer than an hour, while her father cradled me in his arms, trying to comfort me. It has lately become more acceptable, especially in Western society, for men to show their emotions in public. We can thank the women's movement in church and society for liberating men from traditional taboos about showing emotion. Even politicians no longer try to hide their tears. On the contrary, crying at the right time and place might demonstrate sincerity, personal warmth and human concern.

But that was the last thing in my mind on my wedding night. Although in the Asian context, Koreans are regarded as being somewhat less inscrutable than their Chinese or Japanese neighbors, a Korean man was still expected to keep his composure at his own wedding.

A wedding is a time of transition, one of the most profound in one's life. Opening a new chapter in one's life is never easy, particularly if previous chapters have been filled with uncertainties, upheavals and tragedies, as mine had certainly been.

My wedding was a time of grief, as well as celebration. In launching out into a new life, I drew my old life to a conclusion. Up to the day of my wedding, I had been able to avoid confronting the permanent pain that history had dealt me. Then the wedding itself became a symbol, that life moves on relentlessly, no matter what injustice has been done in the past.

At our wedding, all the relatives who surrounded us belonged to my wife. I longed to have my own parents, my two older sisters, my two younger brothers, join me on this important day of my life.

But there was no way to send them an invitation. There was no way to ask them for their blessing on my matrimony. There was no way to know where they were or even if they were still alive. There was no way to tell them that their eldest son, the son to whom the care of the parents in their old age is traditionally entrusted, had taken a wife and started a family of his own. There was no way to say goodbye.

And so I wept, out of guilt for being unable to repay the sacrifice my parents had offered in caring for me; out of frustration for being unable to change the course of history; out of grief for having to bury my past in order to give my new family a future; out of the loneliness of a small boy within me who missed his father and mother so terribly much.

When I left my family in China, I had no idea that I would never see them again. I thought I could return after a few months. Now I was doing the same thing all over again, leaving behind the only family I had and heading for another country. Would this new transition be as dramatic as others had been in my life? What future would Canada hold for me? Would I ever see my wife and children again?

I knew it was pointless to ask such questions. The future is in God's hands.

After telling the stewardess that I wished not to be disturbed, I closed my eyes. Sometimes, looking back over one's past experiences, it is possible to discover reasons and explanations which may not have been apparent at the time. God's guiding hand is never so clear as in retrospect.

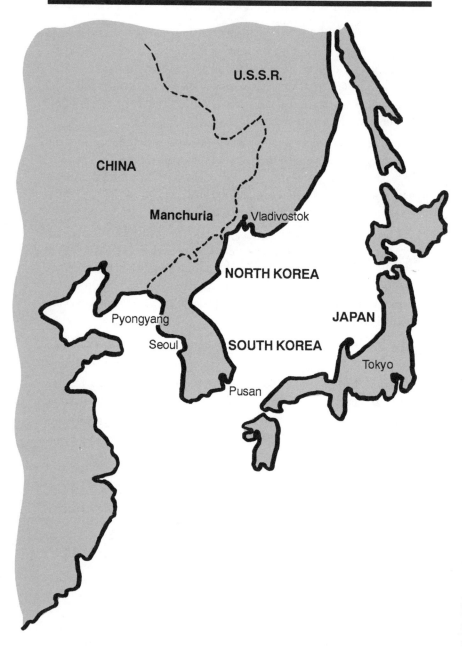

The author had been a refugee in three countries—Siberia, Manchuria, and Korea itself—before coming to Canada

A refugee in Siberia

I do not know the name of the place where I was born. If it had a name, I certainly wouldn't recognize it on a map. It's name was most likely Russian, because I was born in a small farmhouse in Siberia.

My father was a Korean farmer and beekeeper. He took the honey and other farm produce to market in Vladivostok, the Russian empire's eastern-most port city.

The wooden farmhouse we lived in was spacious and comfortable. At least, that is how I remember it. It was home, a place of stability, security, warmth, love, happiness. The front door opened into the largest room, which served as living room, dining room and kitchen. The first door led to the men's bedroom, where my father, his sons, and his hired men slept. The second door led to the women's bedroom, occupied by my mother and two sisters, as well as female guests on those rare occasions when relatives visited.

Furniture was sparse. Chairs were unnecessary, since we sat on the floor for all our activities, including meals. For this reason, our floors were constructed in the Korean fashion, heated from beneath by air from the wood stove at the far end of the main room.

Beyond this kitchen area, without any separating wall, was the stable. This too was a traditional Korean farmers' method of heat conservation. For the first seven years of my life, I found it completely normal to share my living quarters with a horse and a cow, and to have the aromas of supper mingled with stable smells.

My mother, a hardy, determined woman, did not lose a day's work even when she was giving birth. She bore altogether ten children, though only five survived. Of course there were neither hospitals nor doctors—nor even a midwife—anywhere near where we lived, so childbirth involved dangers not only for the newborn, but for the mother as well.

One bitterly cold winter morning, my mother stopped in the middle of her chores to ask my father to take my two sisters to the neighbor and to hurry back. By the time he returned, she had put a kettle of water on the stove, had fetched a bundle of straw from the stable and arranged it before the fire, the warmest place in the house, and had spread a clean sheet over it. My father knew exactly what was expected of him. It was the seventh time he had assisted my mother during a birth.

Later, much later, I would find an intimately personal significance in the story of the birth of the Christ child, lying in a manger, with farm animals in attendance. It wasn't so different from February 29, 1924, when I was born.

Outwitting the gods

I don't remember my parents as particularly religious people. The only religious practice that I was ever aware of in our family always had the same goal—keeping the eldest son alive. I must have been a small and fragile boy.

From the time I was old enough to walk any distance, my father took me for special prayers. Twice a month, on the first and fifteenth day, he wakened me very early in the morning. The first part of the prayer ritual was to wash our bodies thoroughly. This we did in the kitchen area, because of course we had no bath. Nor do I remember using any soap. After this cleansing, we walked up into the mountains.

My father usually carried a bowl of rice and a chicken as offering. We stopped at an enormous tree, which I could recognize from a distance, because it was covered with colorful ribbons and banners. Here, Koreans came to offer prayers and petitions to the gods. My father placed the rice and chicken under the tree. Then made me bow three times with him as he prayed for my life to be spared.

My parents were convinced that the universe was populated by gods and spirits who took great pleasure in bringing misery to ordinary human beings by taking away the lives of their children. Fortunately, my mother's brother was a shaman, and therefore able to offer advice without charging the usual exorbitant fees. He taught my parents the ancient wisdom that evil spirits are not overly endowed with intelligence. They can be tricked. Since they always search for that which is most highly valued by human beings, the best protection is to pretend to despise that which you love the most.

This subterfuge accounted for the variety of names I have carried in my lifetime, including the one by which I am known today.

Four different names

Following my shaman uncle's advice, my first name was "Buokdori"—meaning something like "boy born on the kitchen floor"—indicating a person of no value.

The fact that I survived proved that this trick had worked. My parents worried, however, that even stupid gods cannot be fooled forever. I therefore received a new name, the Russian name "Misha." My parents felt sure that this too was an unflattering name, because it was what a Russian family in that farming area called their dog. They would have been shocked to know that Misha is simply the diminutive of Mikhail, the name given around that same time to a boy later destined to become the leader of the whole Soviet Union!

When the organizers of the Moscow Olympic games in 1980 chose Misha as the name of their mascot teddy bear, I wondered if my parents were still alive. And if they heard about that mascot, and remembered that their first surviving son carried the name Misha until they escaped to China.

I was seven before I received my first proper Korean name. By then, we had taken up a new life in China, and so my father decided we should have new names. Korean names traditionally have three parts. One stands for the family lineage, a second identifies the generation, and the third distinguishes the individuals within that generation.

My father chose the name "Yong," or "dragon" as our generational name. I therefore became "Il-Yong," or "first dragon," and my younger brother "Ee-Yong," or "second dragon." When the next son was born, he became "Sam-Yong," or "third dragon."

When I was about ten or eleven, the shaman told my parents that I was headed for some major crisis, and advised them to give me away.

They were naturally shocked. But the shaman explained that they did not really need to lose me. The spirits have a book of names as a reference.

It was important, the shaman explained, that when the spirits came to our house to fetch Il-Yong, no one by that name live there. To assure this, they could give me up for adoption and have my adoptive parent give me a new name. In that case, of course, Il-Yong would cease to exist, and therefore could not be called to the other world. With another name, as someone else's son, there could be no danger in my continuing to live with my biological family.

Much relieved, my parents began to search for a foster parent who would give me a name, call me "son" and let me call him "father," but make no other claims on me.

The choice my parents made was clever. My new father was a medical practitioner, a traditional doctor who made herbal medicines and used acupuncture, a most respected man in the village. Aside from lending prestige to my family by adopting me, he could be expected to take more than a passing interest in my health!

As it happened, this new parent genuinely liked me. We became friends and I visited him regularly. At times I stayed at his home for weekends. He gave me medical check-ups, and supplied me with medicines when I became ill.

He also gave me my present name—"Sang-Chul."

The only part of my name which remained constant throughout was my family name, Lee. In Korean it is actually pronounced "Ee," and has numerous Western spellings, including Li, Yi and Rhee. I suspect the "Lee" spelling is a transliteration of the Chinese pronunciation of the Korean characters. When Westerners first encountered Koreans, they were already familiar with the Chinese "Lee" and saw no reason to change.

In Korean, the family name is written and spoken first. So my name, properly speaking, is Lee Sang-Chul. In Canada I changed the order to Sang-Chul Lee, because I got tired of being called "Pastor Chul."

In the Confucian tradition, family lineage is very important. Even today, being able to trace your family tree can make a difference in your social standing among Koreans. The Lee family name is one of the oldest, dating back thousands of years. Unfortunately, my father had no documents to prove his lineage. I met only his father, his brother and sister, in Siberia as a child. Other relatives were unknown to me. We heard of other, very distant relatives, but had no way to trace them. This fact put me into an inferior position; it indicated that I belonged to a lower class.

All Lees of Korea, whatever their Western spelling, claim descent from the Yi dynasty, which lasted from the 14th century until Japanese annexation in 1910. Its founder, General Yi Song-Gye, came from what is now Hamgyong Province in the northeast part of Korea. So did my family. Were we descended from the same ancestors, those fierce warriors who distinguished themselves in fighting off Mongol invaders at various times in our early history?

Escape from oppression

I'm not certain exactly when or why my grandfather moved his family from northeastern Korea to Siberia, but I can make some guesses, based on our country's history.

From time immemorial, Korea was a pawn of the powers surrounding it. Whether through hit-and-run attacks by pirates and warlords, through economic domination, or through outright occupation, outside forces have constantly interfered with Korean independence.

In the second half of the 19th century, Japan, taking lessons from European imperialism, became the dominant outside force. Even before official annexation in 1910, the Japanese were able freely to purchase land in Korea. Japanese left their overcrowded homeland to settle in Korea, increasing from only 20,000 in 1897 to over 170,000 in 1910.

As Japanese oppression intensified and annexation neared, more and more Koreans fled abroad. Most of these refugees went by foot to neighboring countries, especially to Manchuria (then in China) and to Siberia on Russia's Pacific coast, where I was born. Northern borders had never been tightly guarded, so many Koreans lived in these areas already. In 1902, according to statistics, about 32,000 Koreans had settled in Siberia. This figure grew to 100,000 by 1910.

If my grandfather had not already left Korea by the time of Japanese annexation, he left soon after. By then, Japan had turned its attention to land ownership. Under the pretext of setting up a modern system of registering land ownership, the Japanese announced a deadline by which all land owners had to report details about their land—such as its location, size, and quality, together with their names and addresses. Many uneducated farmers, not used to such a system, did not understand the meaning of the announcement. Or perhaps they never became aware of it until too late. Others may have decided to refuse to cooperate with the Japanese. The result, as the

Japanese expected, was that many farmers failed to report their information in time, and thus lost the land that their families had worked on for centuries.

The Japanese also seized land when taxes were not paid. Nearly 40,000 Korean family farms were lost by the time the Land Survey ended in 1918.

Land owners like my grandfather had few choices. Those who were too proud to become mere tenants, or to wander aimlessly looking for jobs in the cities, joined the many thousands who had already left Korea to start a new life elsewhere.

I do know that when my grandfather left North Hamgyong Province for Siberia, his three children, two sons and a daughter, must have been teenagers. My father, who was the second son, married my mother in Siberia.

My grandfather, according to Korean custom, lived with my uncle, his oldest son. Therefore I saw him only occasionally. I remember him as a dignified man, proudly wearing traditional Korean costume—the white robe with long, wide sleeves, the black starched hat with a wide brim. I remember being fascinated by the long bamboo tobacco pipe he smoked. As I was later taught, this pipe was a sign of rank. The Japanese had banned both the smoking of such pipes and the wearing of the formal Korean costume in their reform programs, as a means of crushing Korean pride and dignity.

My grandfather's dress suggests to me that he had been a distinguished gentleman, perhaps a leading figure in his home town. He obviously treasured tradition and took pride in being Korean. My memories of this old man are the only link I have with my north Korean ancestry. Whenever I see pictures of men in Korean costume, I see my grandfather.

Family relationships

Education was scarce in those days, especially for Korean refugees. My grandfather did not have the means to put his sons through school. My father received limited schooling through private teachers. My mother had no formal education to speak of.

My father was a quiet, unobtrusive, gentle man. He got along well with his hired workers. With his unassertive character, he had difficulty refusing anything to anyone.

I know that he loved me dearly, and I loved him. I remember going into the fields with him, watching him work, fetching things for him, learning how not to be stung by his bees. He had some 200 hives. And when I did get stung despite his precautions, I could look forward to a taste of honey as an antidote. That was always effective, psychologically if not medically.

His concern for my well-being, including our twice-a-month trip to the mountain for prayers, instilled in me both a sense of worth and of grave responsibility. My parents counted on me, as their oldest son, to care for them in their old age. Someday I would bury them and ensure that coming generations would remember them in their ancestor worship.

Part of the closeness I felt towards my father may also have been due to the fact that we shared the same bedroom throughout my childhood. We were physically close, sleeping under the same blanket. All the hugging or cuddling I remember from my early years came from my father, not my mother.

My mother was a woman of strong character. Though she had practically no education, she had a sharp, logical and organized mind. She taught us right and wrong, and never seemed to have any doubt which was which. She needed to be in control of any situation. She made all the important family decisions. Unfortunately, she also had a sharp temper. Her older brother, the shaman, also had a strong character and a quick temper, so I assume it was a family trait. But this also made it difficult for my mother to express affection.

My mother disciplined us children, and she did so very harshly. Many times we were beaten.

My oldest sister suffered most from this discipline. She received more beatings than the rest of us. I suppose my mother expected the most help from her in running the household. Sometimes, after a beating, my mother would throw her out of the house and forbid her to return for a day or two.

I was particularly fond of my oldest sister. It pained me to see her ejected from the family. I usually found her crying under a tree behind the house. I would bring food to her. Sometimes she talked of suicide. I would cry with her and try, through my presence, to give her some of the love that she missed in the family.

Moments of grief

Two events changed my early perceptions of my mother. Both occurred after we moved to China.

The first was when my oldest sister got married. My mother cried for days. It seemed to me to be a kind of repentance. Or, perhaps, it was simply the sadness any mother feels when her first baby leaves the family forever. In any case, my mother was left with a lot of pain, and this brought me closer to her. She seemed different from that day onwards. She became milder, more considerate, more patient with the rest of us.

The second event was the death of my brother Sam-Yong. Born in China, he became my mother's special boy. He inherited all the character traits of my mother. He was enthusiastic, outgoing, opinionated, venturesome, and got himself into all kinds of trouble, not only at home, but all over the town.

An illness killed him when he was only nine years old. We could not afford a funeral. He was buried without ceremony on the grounds of the farm which we worked.

It was impossible to console my mother when her "Third Dragon" died. Long after his death, she still grieved. She tried to conceal her grief from us. Sometimes, if I woke up in the middle of the night, I could see her by the faint light of the moon, hunched in the corner of the room, weeping quietly into her hands so as not to wake us. Sometimes she slept in the early part of the evening, then after midnight awakened and left the house.

One night I followed her, and found her sitting by my brother's grave. It was shattering to see this strong person, who had so bravely borne the pain of our birth, now so incapable of bearing the pain of our death.

Seeing the bent figure of my mother that dark night in an open field in eastern Manchuria, my heart went out to her in gratitude. At that moment I forgot all the beatings she had given me during my lifetime.

I approached her and knelt down next to her. At my brother's grave, she reached out to me and held me ever so tightly. Her sobs shook my whole body as she rocked me back and forth until dawn lit up the horizon. That night I realized, and I have never doubted since, that she truly loved me.

I have reflected, since then, on how often children fail to realize their parents' love and affection, the bond of their parent's love, until it is too late.

It wasn't until I came to Canada that I began to realize I had inherited more from my mother than I imagined. I had always considered myself more like my father. I was a good boy, I think, but weak, shy, and not the outgoing type. Occasionally I had fights with other boys, but I usually lost. But hiding somewhere within me were my mother's strengths and passions.

My mother had a keen sense of fair-mindedness. When she saw anything wrong, in the family or outside, she had to speak out, even if it risked unpleasantness.

That feeling of justice and the necessity to struggle for what is right I developed in the latter part of my life, when I got seriously involved in issues of human rights. I found that I had a certain stubborn determination which could only have come from my mother.

If only I could reach out to her now and say "Thank you."

Preparing for flight

My mother had more than her share of burdens to bear. The frustrations of refugee life, the pressures of feeding an increasing number of family members, took their toll on my father. He ended up seeking the comfort of alcoholic intoxication. This flaw delayed our departure from Siberia.

The communist revolution had happened in St. Petersburg (Leningrad) and Moscow. But it took time to consolidate its hold over Russian territory. Siberia, especially the eastern part where we lived, did not experience the same sudden transformation as the rest of Russia. This served only to increase our fears about what would happen when communism did reach us, as rumors about atrocities drifted in.

My father believed that we should move to China while the borders were still relatively open. But my mother hesitated. In China the use of opium had reached epidemic proportions. Judging from my father's use of alcohol, my mother feared that he would be drawn into opium use too. Once a person begins to use this narcotic, there is no end to it. The family members of drug users are thrown into abject misery.

And so, despite the denials and promises of my father, my mother bluntly refused to move. "I have no patience to watch you dying from that opium," she told him. And once my mother had made up her mind, the decision was final.

Thus the family remained, waiting to see how the situation would develop. The communist regime became more organized. Opposition forces were gradually eliminated. Many were imprisoned, many suffered execution. Those more fortunate escaped on ships leaving Vladivostok, or were pushed into Manchuria.

A massive educational effort tried to teach the population the principles of communism. Classes were compulsory, of course. It soon became clear to everyone that these study sessions were a form of control. Through them, the authorities could keep track of the population, and discover the dissident elements. It also helped to prevent any real opposition from developing, as there was virtually no time left for people to have meetings of their own.

My parents were not politically active. It was a chore for them to attend these study sessions every evening. Rather than reassuring them of the positive changes communism would bring, the classes merely served to frighten them more.

Rumors, some wildly fabricated, circulated through the Korean community. Though most could be ignored, one rumor frightened my mother enough to change her mind. At one of these evening classes, a particularly gossip-prone Korean neighbor warned my mother that the communist party planned eventually to take children away from their parents.

That night she said to my father, "I can survive living with a drug addict in Manchuria, but I cannot survive without my children."

The decision had been made. My family would escape to China.

Flight into China

My father awakened me gently on the appointed day. It was still pitch dark. He asked me to get dressed quickly and to make no noise. In the family room my parents were busy packing. My oldest sister helped me to get ready. She whispered that we were all going on a long trip to China.

I had no idea what or where China was. I certainly had no idea that it was a trip from which we would never return.

There was a strange man in the stable, untying the horse and cow. Some sacks were already strapped to the horse's back. My brother, still asleep, was settled on the horse as well, in such a way that he would not fall off. I was very excited by this adventure, though my parents and sisters looked worried, even afraid.

The stranger decided we should take a little-used country path. It was so dark that my father carried me on his back to prevent me from stumbling. I looked back. Our house was beginning to disappear in the moonless night. With difficulty I could distinguish the outline of the large willow tree under which I spent so many hours of play. The well near it, from which we drew all our water with a bucket on a string, was no longer visible. The two neighboring houses were but shadows.

In one of them, the only friend I remember clearly from my Siberia days was fast asleep. I do not remember her name. I wonder if she still remembers the boy they called Misha, who disappeared without warning one night, together with his entire family.

There were no farewells. No one could know of our departure. The house was left standing cold and empty. We never knew who took possession of it after we left. My father's 200 beehives had to fend for themselves from that day forward.

The border crossing into Manchuria had become much more difficult as the Soviet authorities consolidated control over this part of Siberia. But though the risks had increased significantly, the flow of refugees continued unabated, with both frightened Koreans and disaffected Russians seeking a new life in China, which itself was in turmoil.

Secrecy was paramount. Everyone was afraid of being reported. Finding one's way through the countryside and across the border was impossible without an experienced guide. As always in times of peril, some people will make a profit out of other people's fears. I do not know how much our guide was paid, but I know that apart from our horse and cow, my parents arrived in China penniless.

I quickly tired of our journey, which took about two weeks. Walking only by night, we set up makeshift camp during the day, under thick trees and bushes. In the early spring it was still very cold at night. The snow was melting, swelling streams and rivers. Rain made walking even more difficult on the wet soil. Often my brother and I had to be carried on the adults' shoulders. Their constant cautions against making noise turned our adventure into a nightmare.

Crossing a river one night, my brother became so frightened, he began to scream. All of us were terrified we would be discovered.

On one occasion, we were almost caught by Russian guards. We must have been near the border. That evening, shortly after setting out, the guide suddenly fell to the ground and signalled us to do the same. I put my hand over my brother's mouth, afraid that he would make a noise. I don't know how my father managed to keep the animals quiet. The soldiers passed, but the guide decided that we would remain in the forest until he could scout another route. We did not continue across the border into China until the next evening.

The end of childhood innocence

My first impression of China was negative. The mountains looked so different from Siberia. The lush green slopes of my former home were replaced by barren crags, with rugged, sparse brush clinging to dusty rocks. I wondered what evil we had committed to be banished to this unfriendly, strange place.

I missed our house and the carefree life I knew there. I missed the security I felt there. Though we were poor by Canadian standards, we had never lacked food or clothing or shelter.

Of course, as a small child I had no idea of the pressures my parents were under at the time. Until we took that journey as refugees, I had never felt the kind of fear emanated by my parents, like the glow of a destructive energy. Though I was just seven years old at the time, our flight from Siberia represented a critical transition in my life. It marked the end of childhood innocence.

A refugee in China

For a couple of weeks we lived in very crowded conditions with an aunt, until my father found work on the farm of a Chinese landowner. We were offered a one-room house (if you could call it that) which became home for the six of us.

There was no such thing as "salary" for the work we did. We had to live on the produce of the land leased to us. Since we had no money any more, my father reluctantly sold the horse. The cow he kept for a longer time. Perhaps it was his souvenir of better times in Siberia.

We had no means of communicating with relatives we left behind. The only news we could get was from occasional refugees arriving later. I still don't know what happened to my grandfather, my uncle, or my cousin.

As a boy of seven, I learned the meaning of work. Manchuria, the province we settled in, at that time was still a part of China. Our whole family, even my younger brother, went into the fields every day. Life was harsh, and food was scarce. Most days we had only rice and water to eat. Occasionally, my mother made "beanjap" when she had beans. "Kimchi," the spicy pickled cabbage Koreans eat with every meal, became ever more rare.

Harvest in Siberia had been a time of celebration and joy. In China, it became a time of despair. I remember vividly that first fall. After a summer of backbreaking work by all of us, we had completed the gathering and storing of our well-earned harvest. One evening at sunset, the landlord came with a large wagon and took away almost all of our harvest. The Chinese had a system called "three and seven." It meant that the landlord had the right to take seventy percent of everything his tenants grew, leaving only thirty percent for them to live on for the following year.

My father, unable to contain himself even in front of strangers, broke into tears. That day I learned the meaning of injustice.

By the following February, we had run out of food. We were forced to borrow food from the landlord—a debt which would increase the landlord's share of crops the following year. In addition, the landlord charged exorbitant interest. We were held in virtual slavery. There was no escape.

I can understand now why my father never stopped drinking alcohol. But to his credit (and probably to my mother's as well), he never started using opium.

Every community had its opium den. Even the small town near us had a building frequented by opium users. In its dark interior, hundreds of people—mostly men—could lie down and smoke the long opium pipes, serviced by the employees of the establishment. After they smoked, they would relax there for two or three hours to forget the miseries of their lives.

Maybe my father never tried opium because of an experience with a seasonal worker on our farm. This man was single and hopelessly addicted to the drug. One winter, on a particularly cold morning, we saw him sitting under a tree on the other side of our house. We went out to invite him to warm himself in the house and take breakfast with us. His emaciated body did not respond. The evening before, after his habitual smoke, he had relaxed and fallen asleep under this tree. During the night, he froze to death.

Working on the roads

With militarists firmly entrenched in the Japanese government, Japan began to prepare for all-out war with China. The first step was the occupation of Manchuria, the part of China where we now lived.

History had come full circle for our family. My grandfather had escaped from the Japanese to Siberia, we had escaped from Russia to China, and now we had come once more under Japanese rule. Ironically, working for the hated Japanese gave us some measure of economic independence.

As Manchuria became the staging ground for the battle for China, the Japanese needed well-built roads for trucks, tanks and military equipment. They needed military compounds, barracks, administration buildings and armories. For my family, these developments provided an escape from the farm. The Japanese wanted energetic laborers, and paid better wages than we could gain on the farm. Our family was transformed into a work brigade.

The Japanese usually contracted out a certain task or a unit of work. Once the task was accomplished, the work crew received an agreed pay. The quicker the work was carried out, the more money could be earned.

Every member of our family participated. I carried stones or other material, as much as I was able. With six of us working strenuously, we could complete assignments fairly quickly. However, we did hard labor incessantly, without rest or free time. And there was no guarantee of continued work at the end of an assignment. Once a construction job was finished, we had to move to another town to look for work, and for a place to live.

My mother taught us to bear our poverty with dignity. She was a practical woman. As always, she organized our lives in such a way that we could cope and, above all, survive.

Whenever possible, need became part of ritual, and thus was made easier to bear. In the early summer, for example, Koreans celebrated a festival called "dano," when we enjoyed one day of rest and recreation. The community organized sporting events, and prepared special food. On this day, our shoes disappeared. Since from then on the weather generally became warmer, my mother hid our shoes. All summer, we went barefoot. Shoes were too expensive to be worn needlessly. Then, at the end of August, with the gathering of the harvest, Koreans celebrated a kind of thanksgiving banquet. On that day, our shoes miraculously re-appeared. In this way, we made a celebration of our poverty.

Although the quality of our lives did not improve with our career in construction, I felt that my parents were glad to be rid of our bondage to the landlord, a bondage which had threatened to swallow up not only our existence, but also our pride. Under these conditions, my mother bore two more sons. Now we were a family of eight.

Education and indoctrination

Like all colonizing nations, Japan was eager to educate its colonies. Japan's experience in Korea made her aware that schools can be a hotbed of resistance. The proud tradition of rebellion among Korean students has recently attained worldwide reputation. But that tradition goes back a hundred years at least.

Japan wanted to prevent the growth of nationalism, not only in Korea itself, but also in Manchuria where many Korean independence groups had set up military operations. As Koreans continued to exit their homeland in great numbers, unable to bear the increasingly brutal Japanese oppression, many were more than sympathetic to the resistance movement.

Japan was well aware that education is also indoctrination. Schools have always been a way for the élite of any nation to perpetuate itself. Both European and Asian colonizers used education as a way to train the disadvantaged and minorities of their colonies for administrative positions, thus harnessing them as collaborators. Also, with an education system controlled by the state, authorities can keep a nation's young under surveillance; they can root out potential trouble-makers while they are still most vulnerable.

And so schools began to appear here and there throughout our territory. In small towns such as the ones we lived in, anyone able to read and write might be drafted to teach the young.

The first school I attended was an ordinary home. There were no tables, no desks, no blackboard. There was no division into classes. Children of all ages sat on the floor and listened to the teacher, the only one with a textbook. For a long time I was the youngest in that group.

Gradually the number of pupils increased, as more people realized that education could improve their children's chances for better jobs, and as more and more Koreans moved into the community.

School was particularly difficult for us Koreans. From the beginning we had to learn not only three languages but three distinct ways of writing. Our teachers, for the most part, were Korean. They taught us Hangul, the Korean alphabet. But since we were under Japanese occupation, we had to learn Japanese as well, which is written in Hiragana. Our surroundings, of course, were Chinese, making the speaking of Mandarin useful. But aside from that, both Japanese and Korean languages still use some 2000 characters of Chinese origin, making the learning of Chinese writing almost essential.

With only the teacher having textbooks, we had to copy all our lessons by hand. The difference between success and failure in school was often determined by the precision and neatness of our handwriting!

But while these difficulties were serious, I enjoyed school. It liberated me from the treadmill of child labor. Far more difficult for me to deal with were the visible signs of my poverty. In school I realized that most other children were better off. At an age when comparisons with peers become all-important for one's self-image, I was tortured by feelings of shame.

Lunch-time was particularly traumatic. All other boys and girls in the school ate together at noontime. But often I had no lunch to bring to school. In my family, breakfast was the main meal, and it had to last the rest of the day. So on most days I sneaked out of class at noon and sadly kicked around stones on the grounds, pretending to be content while others ate.

Eventually, as education became more organized, teachers began to charge fees. This presented new hardships. Often the teacher would send home those who were unable to pay. We were told not to come back to school if we could not afford the fees. When my parents explained to me that there simply was no money, I went back to school anyway and begged the teacher to allow me back into the class.

Inside, my heart was breaking. Who was I to blame for my misfortune? My parents, I knew, were doing everything within their power. Other parents might have put me back to work. Nor could I blame the Japanese. Was it not the Japanese who encouraged education and provided my parents' livelihood? The Chinese were able to resign themselves to fate. But I was not Chinese. I was Korean. And Koreans—this I somehow felt instinctively—do not resign. Koreans struggle.

Were the gods to blame? The only gods I knew as yet were the devils who play havoc with people's lives. But they were never very real to me. I had not yet heard about the Christian God, the one God, all-powerful, with infinite wisdom. Otherwise I would have known on whom to unload my frustration and despair.

First experiences of repression

As they had in Korea, the Japanese replaced civilian police in Manchuria with their own military police. Our surroundings became more and more militarized. These officers also had to guard roads and forests, protect the mails, enforce tax collection, and even oversee the spread of the Japanese language. And as I was to discover in a frightening way in my early school days, they also had the task of repressing Korean independence movements.

One day a Japanese policeman came to our classroom and ordered all the pupils to line up in the courtyard. In the distance we could see a long line of people walking one behind the other, approaching the school. As they came closer, we saw blood on their faces. About 30 men and women halted in front of the children. Only then we realized that all of them were attached to each other by a long string threaded through holes cut into their ears.

The policeman explained that these were members of the outlawed independence movement. He called them criminals. He implied that if we Korean children did not obey the Japanese authorities, our parents might find themselves in the same situation. Our class was totally quiet and subdued for the rest of the afternoon.

Unfortunately, this was only the first of many even more terrifying experiences of intimidation.

One day the entire village was ordered to the outskirts of the town, where a man was digging a hole. I stood next to my father, who had a firm hand on my shoulder. He knew what was about to happen. I could feel the fear and tension of the whole community, gathered in silence.

A military officer gave a lecture—the same basic lecture about the illegality of resistance against the Japanese authorities which I would hear many times over the years—while the condemned man knelt before his own freshly-dug grave. In retrospect, I have a deep sense of respect for this man, who faced his executioners without a whimper. His quiet courage offered a far more powerful statement than the officer's lecture.

The long, sharp sword blade descended swiftly, severing the head in one stroke. A fountain of blood erupted.... I did not see the body follow its head into the grave, because I had buried my face in my father's breast.

As Japanese impatience with Korean independence movements increased, such "examples" became more frequent. On one occasion, I watched a dozen people executed. Two of them were women. This was particularly disturbing. As a child I could not imagine a woman doing anything so terrible as to deserve such a fate.

I began to realize the victims were always Koreans. We developed an inarticulate feeling—which grew clearer as time passed—that somehow we were an inferior people. Though our teachers were all Koreans, teaching of Korean culture and history was not permitted. On the other hand, Japanese superiority was demonstrated again and again simply by brute force.

Nonetheless, on countless occasions, our teachers did give us some hints, some "handles" by which to evaluate the situation and our place in it. One incident in particular, etched permanently into my memory, revealed to me the inner values that we Koreans had to cultivate in order to assert our dignity.

I cannot remember exactly what started it. Probably it resulted from negligence in doing homework, or inattention during the class. At any rate, our teacher began to lecture us, becoming increasingly emotional, until he finally broke into tears.

"What kind of future do you have as Koreans?" he asked us. "The Japanese see us merely as savages. They call us lazy. If we do not work hard, how can we prove them wrong about us? We can only live with pride if we stand up for ourselves and better ourselves. No one else will do it for us."

That outburst, spoken with such emotion, gave us all kinds of messages. I remember that we all cried or were close to tears that day. We were ashamed about our attitude and came away valuing our Korean identity just a little more. We also came away feeling a little more bitterness towards the Japanese. Only much later did I understand the risk this teacher had taken in giving us such a lecture.

Finally, one event eliminated all remaining doubts about the way justice was being administered.

My oldest sister had married at 16. Her husband was a handsome young man of 18. I was very fond of him. In fact, my sister enlisted my aid in soliciting our parents' permission; I begged them to allow the marriage to proceed. Tragically, the marriage lasted only a short time. One day my sister's husband was shot by the Japanese, along with 15 others. After his arrest, she had been refused permission to see him. She was not warned of his impending execution; she was unable to give him any last farewell. After the victims were killed, they were buried in a mass grave whose location was kept secret. Family members were warned not to try to locate the place.

It took me a long time to recover after this tragedy. I sorely missed that young man, and dearly loved my sister. After years of unhappiness at home, she deserved this relationship which appeared to hold so much promise. To make matters even worse, she was pregnant at the time. Her baby girl died a short time after birth.

In my heart, I knew that my brother-in-law could have done no wrong. If this could happen to him, then none of us Koreans were safe, no matter how we behaved ourselves.

It was a rude awakening. I began to reflect seriously about what might become of my life. Gradually I engaged my father in conversation. Though he spoke little, I gathered some stories about my grandfather. I came to realize that Japanese oppression had now reached the third generation of our family. Anger and fear, frustration and despair, competed in my mind and my emotions. How could I overcome what had already defeated my father and his father before him?

Starting a new school

When I reached Grade 6, our school acquired two professionally qualified teachers. Their task was to upgrade the educational level of our school to approximately Japanese standards. For a month they subjected us to all kinds of tests. At the end of that time, they invited all parents and pupils together for a consultation.

After a lengthy explanation about the inferior quality of education in our town, and how all this would have to be changed for our own good, they announced that all of us were being downgraded two years. Not a single exception would be made for my entire class of about 30 boys and girls.

Needless to say, we were all quite distressed. Two grades meant the loss of two years that could have been used for the benefit of my family.

I discussed this situation with a number of my friends, and found nine others who did not wish to accept this decision unchallenged. We decided to appeal to our teacher to take us down only one grade, rather than two. Our begging was of no avail. The teacher denied our appeal categorically. He tried to convince us that this was for our own good, that we would learn more this way. We could not accept his reasoning.

One of my friends had heard of another school in a neighboring town, about one hour's walking distance away. Perhaps we would find more leniency there.

When the ten of us found the school after a long walk, it appeared to be in much better shape than ours! We began to fear that their standards might be beyond our reach.

Upon meeting the principal, our hearts sank even further. He was a stern man, who gave the impression that we were imposing on his precious time. We explained our situation. He said not a word until we had finished. Then he called a teacher to put us through some tests in reading and mathematics. To our immense surprise and gratification, the results were good enough to admit us into Grade 6.

With great excitement we reported our good fortune to our parents that night. Going to this new school meant an early start every morning and an hour's walk each way, but we considered this a minor sacrifice for regaining two years out of our lives.

Strange rituals

All ten of us set out very early the next morning. None of our families owned a clock or watch, so we had to guess the time from the rising of the sun. That first morning, as for many mornings to come, we met and took the journey together as a group. It was more fun that way, and ensured that none of us would oversleep.

The school building was a large open room, divided into three classes by means of curtains. When we arrived, the curtains were separated and all the students were sitting together. The stern principal stood at the front and said some words. Everyone rose to their feet and sang a song we had not heard before. A teacher read from a book, and then the principal gave a talk. Though he spoke Korean, I had difficulty understanding his meaning.

At the end of his talk, all the students rose to their feet. Then something even stranger happened. The teacher said some words which again I could not understand. But they must have been a command, because at that moment the whole student body fell to their knees on the ground. Only the ten of us were left standing awkwardly, glancing at each other in confusion. The period ended by everyone shouting loudly what sounded like "oomah!" One of my friends later likened it to the sound made by a herd of cattle!

On the way home that evening, the ten of us had an animated discussion about our first day's adventure, particularly the first class. There was something rather odd about this school, we were certain. Fortunately, the rest of the day had proceeded in a normal way, so we felt reassured.

We made a pact that we would try to avoid attending that abnormal class, should it recur. We soon realized that the same peculiar ritual was repeated every morning. From that point onward, we took turns as scouts— and managed always to arrive exactly at the conclusion of morning devotions.

First contact with Christian missions

We did not realize it at that time—nor did we care—that we had just made our first contact with Christianity. A sign on the building indicated that this school was operated by the Methodist church. But that fact was meaningless to us. So was the fact that this building became a parish sanctuary on Sundays, except that we could stay home one day a week.

The school's principal was the Methodist pastor, a Korean who had served as a military officer before the Japanese disbanded the Korean army. He ran the school like a military academy, where orders were given and obeyed without question, with little time wasted on clarifying why things were done that way.

This explains how—in spite of the fact that I attended a Christian school for a whole term—I was not much wiser about the content of Christianity. I heard the names of Jesus and God, but they seemed to have nothing to do with me.

The conclusion of our stay in the Methodist school proved even more peculiar than the beginning. In March, a few days before our graduation, the principal called the ten of us into his office. He ordered us to appear in church the coming Sunday morning at 11 o'clock.

Unwilling to risk insubordination so close to graduation, all ten of us showed up on time. The church elders met us, oozing kindness and warmth,

and guided us to the very front. We could almost feel the congregation's smiles and stares in our backs.

The worship service itself seemed similar to morning devotions on school days. We wondered why we had to endure this on a Sunday. Then near the end of the proceedings, the principal asked us to stand in front in a straight line. Our embarrassment caused some of us to blush. I was glad that at least we did not have to face the crowded room. After more words and intimidating responses, we were told to kneel on the floor. Having had numerous opportunities to observe how this was done, we all obeyed.

Yet we were quite unprepared for what happened next. The principal approached us, while an elder next to

Lee Sang-Chul, graduating from Grade 6, clutching his diploma.

him held a container with water. Saying the same strange words repeatedly, the principal reached into the container and sprinkled water over each of our heads in turn.

This ritual was too bizarre for our youthful sensibilities. When a spray of water landed on the first boy, he twitched with such surprise that the rest of us choked with amusement. Each time the procedure was repeated, our merriment increased. Though we tried valiantly, we found it impossible to suppress our giggles.

On the way home, ignoring the spring flowers valiantly pushing their petals into the dusty air alongside the dirt road, we exploded into waves upon waves of laughter. We had no idea that we had just been baptized into the Christian Church.

Higher education

Only one of my ten friends, a boy named Kang, had parents rich enough to send their son to high school. I myself joined the working world again. Without any training, I had to take whatever work I could find. I shined shoes, I cleaned offices, I did odd jobs. Whatever money I earned, I dutifully submitted to the family budget.

Yet my parents never tired of advising me to continue my education. They told me they would make whatever sacrifices were necessary to allow me to go back to school.

This I could not accept. I was the oldest son. How could I spend my parents' hard-earned money, causing my family further hardships for the sake of my own self-improvement? I wanted to return to school, but it had to be by my own means.

After two years, my parents told me there was now enough money for me to go. What is more, the money was all mine. They had never touched a single penny of the little money I had earned, but held it in safekeeping for this day. I vowed that I would make them proud of me.

I chose the school attended by my friend Kang. He was entering Grade 9 when I started Grade 7. This school was located in a much larger town. At that time we called the town by the Korean name of Yong Jung, though today it is a city with the Chinese name of Loong Jing. I had to take the train to reach it. My friend, who lodged in a private home paying for his room and board, was eager to have me move in with him.

There were six high schools in Yong Jung, four for boys and two for girls. Each school was sponsored or backed, overtly or covertly, by different factions. One had a strongly nationalistic background, with close connections to the independence movement; a second had connections with Korean communists; a third was Christian; the fourth pro-Japanese. For girls, there was a Christian and a pro-Japanese school.

Though Manchuria was in China, the large majority of Yong Jung's inhabitants were Korean. (Even today, the part of China bordering Korea has only a minority of Chinese inhabitants.) We even called the section of town where most of the Chinese lived "Chinatown," as though we were in some other country. Yet by the time I went to school there, the Japanese had prohibited Korean as a teaching language. Speaking only Japanese in classrooms, we soon became fluently bilingual.

On my first day of school, I was surprised to discover that classes here opened with the same kind of ceremony as in the Methodist school. What surprised me even more was the lusty way my friend Kang participated!

That evening I teased him about his performance. "You never liked to attend that funny period back home in primary school," I said. "What happened to you here?" He confessed that he had become a Christian. He had become an active participant in church activities and was devoted to the study of the Bible. Moreover, he encouraged me strongly to join him and become a Christian myself.

Nothing could have been further from my mind. I was young, in search of a direction for my life. There were too many ideas to explore, too many worlds to discover, too many tumultuous questions occupying my mind.

Intellectual ferment

If clarity of mind was my goal, I could not have come to a worse place. With so many schools, Yong Jung provided a lively intellectual atmosphere. It was also a place where every conceivable stream of Korean political thought intersected. I found my mind pushed and pulled, tossed and turned, in many directions at the same time.

The leadership of many movements passed through this town at one time or another, often in secrecy because of Japanese surveillance. The town was a spawning ground for political, social and religious leaders who became prominent in both North and South Korea following the Second World War.

For me it was also the place where I had my first intimate contacts (apart from the Russian farmers in Siberia) with non-Asian foreigners. The principal of my school was George Bruce, a Canadian. There was no way I could have known then how providential his nationality would turn out to be. Our school, along with the Christian girls' school, a hospital, a nurses' training school and a Bible school, was operated by The United Church of Canada Mission Board.

At this Canadian church outpost, I met a number of young Korean Christians who would later make significant contributions to human rights and democracy in South Korea. These included such well-known personalities as the Rev. Kang Won-Yong, who later founded the Christian Academy in South Korea, the Rev. Moon Dong-Hwan, and his brother Moon Ik-Hwan, an oft-arrested minister who became a member of South Korea's first democratically elected parliament in 1988, and several others.

For a while, the communist way of thinking offered certain attractions. I was sick and tired of the poverty that had taken its toll on my family. I had witnessed the injustice of the rich landlord, who could extract blood from his hopelessly indebted farmers without any pity or pangs of conscience. I had seen the cruelty and repression of a military imperial system. There must be other, more equitable ways of organizing society's relationships, I was certain. The communists seemed to offer an alternative.

Yet I also knew that my parents left a more comfortable life in Siberia to avoid communism. Something about communism frightened them.

My attraction to communism, as I later realized, was based entirely on negative emotions. I hated rich people. I found them cruel, distasteful, nasty. I was angry at them. I was jealous of them. But negative reactions to negative experiences do not necessarily produce positive results. I hungered for positive values, for hope, and the communism I had encountered did not satisfy that hunger.

I became an avid reader. I devoured books as a starving person devours food. I could not get enough. I raided the school library repeatedly. When I got into a good book, I sacrificed my sleep to complete it. I even skipped classes to read.

My reading increased my sensitivity to the independence movement. Practically all prominent Korean writers in this period were nationalists. Traditional Korean literature, largely influenced by China, had stagnated with the decline of the Chinese empire. Under Japanese domination, a "New

Literature Movement" provided Koreans with pride in themselves. Much of this literature appeared in novel form, which made it even more exciting for young readers like me. I particularly loved books by Yi Kwang-Su. Some critics called his work "sermon literature." But precisely this social orientation appealed to me.

By this time, Japanese control had become almost absolute. With the establishment of the "Manju Dynasty," a Japanese puppet government, in 1932, freedom of expression was nearly obliterated. Writers turned to the rural scene, advocating a return to nature, a retreat from contemporary society into local color and customs.

One of the novels of Yi Kwang-Su from that period, titled "Huk," (meaning "Earth") dealt with a young university graduate who retreated to the countryside after repeated harassment from the Japanese police. He took up farming and began to educate local boys and girls, eventually becoming a catalyst for development in the area. The community became organized; schools, churches, cooperatives were created.

Although this concept appealed to me, there was also something alienating about it. The main figures in these novels, like the writers themselves, all seemed to belong to the middle or upper levels of Korean society. They were people with names, with family registers, who cared for the poor. But they were not part of the poor. Their dreams were pleasant, luxurious even, but somehow out of touch with the reality I had experienced.

Reading these novels, nevertheless, had two significant results.

The first was that I began to ask different questions. The fact that the people in these novels found ways to contribute to the happiness of the larger community appealed to me. They gave of themselves to others. To this point, I had searched only for a way to improve my own life, to climb out of the rut of poverty into which my parents had fallen.

From then on, instead of worrying about my own life, I began to ask where, or to what, or to whom, I could offer myself.

The second result was that I also began to read Christian authors, and found their work to be an exhilarating discovery. Although he later converted to Buddhism, Yi Kwang-Su was Christian when he wrote the novels I read. This led me naturally and logically to other Christian authors.

Discovering Christianity

The author who really got me hooked on Christian literature was the Japanese saint Toyohiko Kagawa. As the child of the mistress of a rich man, he had no social status in Japanese society. He was a nobody. His mother could not even register his name.

When he grew up, Kagawa became a Christian. One day he became very sick. The doctors diagnosed his illness as tuberculosis. He was told he had a maximum of three months to live. In despair, he went to his room and began to pray. How could he use his last three months most effectively?

He ended up going to one of the worst slums in Japan's cities. There he taught evening classes to factory workers. He helped the homeless and prostitutes. As Japan had no social services at that time, his work load expanded. His three months came to an end, but he felt better than he had before in his life. Miraculously, he had been cured. He became a minister.

Kagawa's books were eye-openers. I could identify with his origins at the bottom of the social scale, but I was amazed that he would selflessly offer his last months of life to others. Until then, I had thought it natural—especially for the poor—to expend all their energies on their own survival.

There was something radically different about this person. My curiosity was aroused. There seemed to be a common thread emerging among all the Christians I was reading. I had to find out more. Who was this Jesus Christ that so impressed all of them?

As I soon discovered, there was no shortage of books about Jesus in the school library. I eagerly read many of them, but found them disappointing.

The Jesus they described—a pious, saintly, almost ghost-like holy man, somewhat innocuous and out of touch with the realities I knew—was not one to whom I could easily relate. The excitement I had found in Kagawa's books was lacking.

Then I decided to tackle the Bible itself. My friend Kang, thrilled by my new interest in Christianity, suggested I start with the Gospels. It took some effort to overcome my resistance to the writing style of this book, and there was much I could not understand. The cultural setting was totally foreign to me. But some passages read as simply as if they were written for children.

I became more familiar with this Jesus person. He was poor, like me. He was harassed and persecuted, just as we Koreans were. Yet he cared for others, loved them, helped them, healed them. And finally he was put to death, though he had committed no crime, just like my brother-in-law.

After the Gospels, I tried Paul's letters, but I could make little sense of them. The strangeness I had felt in those Grade 6 morning devotions returned. I stopped reading Paul.

Then I decided to try some earlier parts of the Bible, and discovered the amazing world of the Old Testament.

The story of Moses was a revelation. The children of Israel suffering under the unjust oppression of Egypt seemed exactly like the Koreans under the Japanese. The story echoed in me. Sometimes I could not sleep. I had to read it over again and again. The God described in these passages did not try to get the better of mortals, like the gods my parents had tried to appease. This God _helped_ people in their struggle. He _liberated_ them. Perhaps he could do the same for all of us.

It dawned on me that the Bible did not see things in a static way, as did Confucianism, for example, or the Shintoism of Japan. The Christian God seemed always to change history. This meant that tomorrow things do not have to be as they are today. There is reason for hope. The retreat from struggle that I had found in contemporary Korean literature was not the only option.

What is more, this Christian Bible seemed to value people without regard to their origins or social status. It placed a value on the poor, the sick, the downtrodden, the defeated. A man cruelly executed as a criminal gets called the Son of God.

It was an utterly crazy concept. But I liked it. I hungered for more.

Surprised by the church

My friend Kang was so excited about the changes in my attitude towards Christianity that he began to bug me to come to church with him. My interest so far had been mainly intellectual; I saw no need for me to get involved in rituals. But I gave in, feeling that if I paid attention to the sermons, I might learn more about the Bible.

What I learned, instead—and have continued to learn throughout my life—is that God is full of surprises. I had looked forward to the sermons, thinking I would be bored by the service. In fact, I was bored by most of the sermons. But something in the service changed my life.

I discovered prayer.

For people who have never witnessed a Korean prayer meeting, this may be hard to understand. Korean Christians pray fervently, loudly and at great length. In their prayers they pour out all the concerns that weigh heavily on their hearts, in full expectation that God will listen and respond. During a church service, if the minister asks the people to pray, the whole congregation will pray spontaneously and simultaneously, but not silently. They all voice their concerns in their own words, at the same time, out loud. In a large church such prayer can sound like the roar of ocean waves smashing against the shore during a storm. It can send shivers up and down your spine.

The first time I heard such a prayer, I thought it must have been the sound heard by the children of Israel when Moses parted the sea, or the sound of the mighty rushing wind on the day of Pentecost. I watched all these people, listening to the cacophony of voices, without saying anything myself. I didn't yet know how to pray, or even whether I wanted to. But I knew something powerful was happening here, something which took hold of people. I felt myself swept up in it. It was frightening, but it felt good.

I don't recall at what point I myself began to pray. The date and time are irrelevant anyway. Even before I spoke on my own, I participated in the prayers of others. My friend prayed for me, and much of what the pastor or the congregation prayed was relevant to me. When I did join in, it was merely a natural extension of my prior involvement to put my own words to the prayers which had captured my heart.

I had a thousand things to pray for. A lifetime of longing, hunger, confusion, frustration, anger, anxiety, fear, pain, sorrow, worry, loneliness and guilt waited to find expression in those prayers. Prayer for me was not so much petitioning God for favors as sharing the despair that had been such a part of my life.

And in the process of sharing, I experienced a miraculous cleansing. I felt somehow renewed, uplifted, blessed. These words, which I had never understood, though Christians loved to use them, gathered meaning through my prayer experiences. My outlook on life became more positive. I felt that I was no longer alone. I began to see some hope for the future.

Starting over as a Christian

I don't know when exactly I began to consider myself a Christian. There was no single dramatic or miraculous moment of conversion. Prayer simply became more and more a part of my life. I never ran out of things to put before God. I would pray for hours and hours at a time, pouring out my soul.

Sometime during all this, I realized that my readings and my prayer were coming together. Somehow I began to see who Jesus really is, and felt him very near to me. When I was in church, praying loudly with all those assembled there, I felt the presence of the Spirit of God, and it came to me that I was speaking not to some foreign God imported from Canada, but to my own God, who loved me.

I became a devoted Christian. I attended prayer meetings every morning at 5 o'clock. I went to church not only on Sundays, but during many evangelical campaigns which ran nightly. It was an exciting time. I could not get enough of religion.

The author
as a young man

I became so engrossed in the charismatic aspects of my Christian life that for some time my earlier social concerns were pushed into the background. There were exceptions, of course. Some of my seniors, such as Kang Won-Yong, encouraged me to read literature which helped to enlighten me. He and some others, who became close friends and colleagues in later years, were already attending university in Tokyo. They came home during holidays, bringing with them fresh ideas and literature.

Evangelistic meetings usually invited special guests to preach. These speakers were often stimulating. Some used Old Testament texts, including the prophets, and their sermons contained subtle insights which fired my imagination. It became clear to me, though, that preachers had severe restrictions in what they could preach during this period. They could not be very direct. Religious organizations were carefully watched by the Japanese, who suspected Christians of infecting Koreans with Western ideas about nationalism and democracy.

Occasionally, pastors were subjected to harassment and imprisonment. On one occasion, after preaching to us for a week, an evangelist left for his home in another town. Three days later, his wife came looking for him. He had not yet returned. Our pastor made inquiries, and found him in a prison cell in the local police station. He had been tortured. He was accused of instigating Korean independence in his sermons. An agent had monitored his sermons. The evangelist was released after two weeks in jail, but only after further torture as a warning not to continue his line of preaching.

I remember being thrilled about this man's sermons on some of my favorite texts from the stories of Moses. But the Old Testament had become a red flag to the Japanese. Near the end of the Second World War, Japanese authorities tried to prohibit any teaching of the Old Testament in colleges.

Even Japanese preachers were harassed, beaten and arrested—though their Japanese citizenship afforded them somewhat greater protection, as St. Paul's Roman citizenship had during biblical times. One of these Japanese preachers, the Rev. Oda (his Korean name was Chun Yong-Bok), insisted on preaching to Koreans in Korean language, and openly criticized Japanese persecution of Koreans.

These incidents taught me that although the church often seemed very conservative, some Christians and pastors were sensitive to the aspirations of my people. On such occasions, my prayers became even more emotional. In these moments, I became sure that I could offer myself in service to the Christian church.

Parental disagreement

My parents were not happy about my decision to become a Christian. They had moved to Yong Jung to be with me, and tried hard to dissuade me.

For my part, I tried equally hard to impress them with Christianity through my own behavior. I became an obedient and faithful son in every respect. I helped at home every way I could think of, remaining cheerful, acting as a good elder brother to my siblings. In fact, they did notice the positive changes in me. But I had no hopes that my parents or brothers and sisters would join me in my conversion. As far as I know, none ever did.

One night I awakened from sleep and heard my parents quietly discussing me. I was the oldest son. The family inheritance and responsibilities would pass to me. I would be responsible for carrying on the family traditions, including the duty of ancestor worship. Yet how could I fulfill these duties if I was now a Christian?

Finally they said, "What can we do? He is old enough to make his own decision. We tried to reason with him, but we see no sign that he will change his mind." They concluded that it was time to accept the inevitable and to stop bothering me about it. From then on the subject was not mentioned again.

The wisdom of God

By this time I understood the meaning of baptism. It bothered me that my own baptism had happened without my consent, when I knew little about its meaning, and had no loyalty whatever to the Christian church. I felt the need to validate my new commitment. So I asked my pastor to re-baptize me, to make it official. He told me he wanted time to think about my request before giving me an answer.

When he talked to me again later, he told me that it was not necessary for me to be baptized a second time. "You didn't know clearly what was happening with you back then," he explained, "but God knew everything." My decision to become a member of the Christian church, he told me, validated that first baptism. I was already one of God's own.

That simple comment, "You didn't know... but God knew everything," impressed and moved me. I never forgot that conversation.

"You didn't know, but God knew." My whole life has become a proof of the truth of that statement.

Tortured and betrayed

Those were tumultuous years. After launching its war with China in

1937, Japan swept into Southeast Asia. When France fell in 1940, Japan invaded Indochina and Thailand, pretending to liberate the Asian people from Western colonialism. That same year, Japan concluded a military alliance with Nazi Germany and Italy; the following year it attacked the American fleet at Pearl Harbor.

During this heady period of victories, Japan became ever more repressive against Koreans in Korea. This naturally spilled over into the Korean parts of China. Young people had to mature very rapidly. I had witnessed brutality before, of course, but as still a teenager I experienced it first hand. With a terrible abruptness, I became an adult.

At our school, some ten of us, aged from 15 to 17, wanted to improve our grasp of the Korean language. For about a year we met every Sunday afternoon in the basement of the church to study Korean grammar, vocabulary, and proper writing and speaking. We had no political purposes. We did not discuss independence or the Japanese occupation. We planned no acts of disobedience. Even the literature we used was innocuous.

But at a time when Koreans were even forced to adopt Japanese names, striving for literacy in our native language was considered subversive. One Sunday afternoon, our basement room was suddenly raided by what seemed like the whole local police force. All of us were taken into custody.

At the police station, we were thrown into a dark and filthy cell. It was permeated by an acrid stench of urine that I could not get accustomed to. At night we slept on the dirt floor, plagued by mosquitoes and insects that crawled from the cracks in the walls to feast on us. We developed sores from scratching ourselves, with no opportunity to clean our wounds.

Each dawn brought other fears. We were called individually to the interrogation room, where we were kicked, beaten, slapped and knocked around, while the same questions were repeatedly fired at us: "What is your connection to the independence movement?" We often wished we could tell them something, so they would stop beating us. But as we were innocent, we could tell them nothing.

Worse than both insects and beatings for me was one fact—the interrogator was not Japanese, but Korean like myself. Like all colonists, the Japanese used local people for their dirty work whenever possible. I was ashamed to discover that Koreans could be traitors to their own people.

Our tormentor was a small man, in both body and mind. I hated him. It was the first time in my life that I really experienced the power of hatred. I

had known of other collaborators, informers, or businessmen and adminis-
trators who managed to enrich themselves by exploiting their own kind. I
had considered them deserving only contempt. But for this interrogator,
who seemed to enjoy his borrowed power over us, for this practitioner of
violence who sold his integrity to the enemy, I developed a loathing that ate
me up inside.

We were released without charge two weeks after our arrest. The
exercise had accomplished its purpose. We no longer studied Korean, and
every student in the school would henceforth be aware of the risks of
stepping even slightly out of line.

Conscription comes

We heard of Japan's expansion into the Pacific in 1942, driving the
Americans out of the Philippines and the British out of Hong Kong and
Singapore. We did not hear about the battle of Midway Island when that
mad expansion came to a halt.

But we knew that millions of Koreans were being forced to work in
mines and factories, and that phenomenal amounts of rice and other produce
were being exported from Korea to Japan while Koreans starved. We did not
hear that the Japanese war machine had spread itself too thinly, and that
shortages afflicted their own supply lines.

We certainly learned of a new law that Korean young men were now to
be drafted into the Japanese army. There would be no exemption or dispen-
sation. Koreans would be sent to far-off places to fight in a war of aggres-
sion which they did not begin and from which they could not benefit. It was
clear to us that Korean soldiers in the army would be the first to die. We
would be placed at the front lines, in the most vulnerable positions. It was
clear also that few could escape the draft. The Japanese administration was
run so efficiently that police had detailed records about everyone which
followed us wherever we went.

The prospect of military service took a terrible toll among young
Koreans. Some committed suicide. Many gave up their studies. Some tried
to flee into the mountains to hide. Others turned to drink and delinquency.

As for me, I went to church every morning and prayed that God would
spare me. Repeatedly, I promised God, "If you save me from this threat, I
will dedicate my life to you." I didn't really know what this meant, nor what
God would do with me, should my prayers be answered. I never considered

that death might not be the only fate which could separate me from my family forever.

A fifth name

During this time, the Japanese forced Koreans to adopt Japanese names. Many with Lee as their surname, like my parents, chose "Miyamodo" or "Kunimodo." "Miya" stands for "palace," "kuni" for "nation," and "modo" for "origin," indicating that the Miyamodo and Kunimodo families are of royal descent, a reference to the Yi dynasty. I was not convinced that these names suited me. I did not feel connected to royalty.

In my inner struggles about being drafted, I confronted a range of fears. Cruel and aggressive military officers hated Koreans, and particularly Christian Koreans. If they knew I was a Christian, they would surely try to destroy my faith. An even greater fear was that I might not have the strength to remain loyal to Jesus. I wanted a name that would constantly remind me of being a Christian.

Finally I chose the fifth name of my short life. I chose "Kanda" as my surname. "Kan" means "God" and "da" means "field." To this I added the personal name "Sukio," "suki" standing for "plough" and "o" for "farmer." Kanda Sukio therefore meant a farmer with his plough in the field of God. I prayed that God would protect Kanda Sukio during military service, that I would have the strength of faith to overcome temptation and never be permitted to betray God.

Working for the war

After graduation, my first job was with a Japanese company building an airport in northern Manchuria, near the Russian border. I no longer had to endure the hardships of construction labor myself, because in school I had acquired some skills in civil engineering. I was part of a group responsible for surveying and checking construction to make sure that plans were being precisely followed.

I thought I had already seen misery in my lifetime, but what I found there surpassed even my imagination. The construction labor force consisted of 2,000 Chinese coolies. They lived in sub-human conditions. Their food was insufficient, of poor quality, and provided only sporadically, since the war effort had priority for all supplies. Their clothes, if they had any, were pitiful. New clothes and shoes were rare, and of such poor quality that they quickly wore out. Most coolies worked in their bare feet and many were absolutely naked.

Japanese overseers treated these Chinese harshly, beating them if they rested or collapsed. As that summer of 1944 wore on, many became ill and died on the job. I took pity on them, remembering the years my own family had worked on construction. I treated those desperate men gently. Whenever I could, I tried to say a kind word.

After some months on this job, I was invited to dinner at the house of a local Chinese leader. He was quite rich, an owner of land and head of the coolies on the project. I felt honored and grateful for the marvellous dinner I was served.

"How long are you planning to stay here?" he asked me after some hours.

"I am fortunate to have this job," I replied. "The company is a good one. I am paid a decent wage. I will stay until we finish the project."

He looked at me for some time, then said, "If I were you, I would go home as soon as possible."

I was puzzled. I asked him why he gave me such advice. He took some time to explain, but he made his points so obliquely that I wasn't quite sure I understood what he was getting at. He may have noticed that, because after some more rice wine, he suddenly blurted out, "Why is a fellow like you being so faithful to the Japanese here?"

Something clicked in my mind. "Are you telling me that the war is coming to an end?" I asked.

He nodded. There was no way the Japanese could sustain their war effort, he told me. There were shortages of everything. The supply lines were running dry. The Japanese would soon lose the war, and then everything would collapse for them, including their colonies.

I asked him why he was telling me this. Was he aware that he was taking a great risk, since I worked with the Japanese? What he told me then moved me deeply and proved to me that Jesus Christ's way of love and kindness is the best.

Yes, he told me, he knew exactly what he was doing. The coolies working on the project had gossiped about me. They could not distinguish between Japanese and Koreans, especially since we all had Japanese names now. But somehow, my behavior impressed them as different from the others. I never kicked them or beat them. When I addressed them, I spoke kindly and with respect. I tried to be nice to them. They wondered why.

As time passed, word reached this leader. He began to watch me. He found out that I was Korean. From then on he had sympathy for me, and decided to give me this warning. If I stayed until the end of the war, he told me, I would be in danger.

I had no idea that the end of the war was close. But when I contacted friends who had links with the independence movement, they confirmed his news, and urged me to go home immediately. I took their advice.

When the war ended, a rebellion by the coolies killed a number of Japanese working on the project. Others were taken to labor camps in the Soviet Union. The old Chinese leader had saved my life. In hindsight, I realized that plans for a rebellion had already been prepared, and he wished to spare me.

For the rest of my life, I never forgot this lesson; it has served me well even in my life in Canada. If you treat people with humanity and civility, listen to them, encourage them, then they will see God through you.

I believed, or at least hoped, that this was a sign that God was answering my prayers. I had not yet heard from the conscription authorities, though many other Korean youths had already been sent to military training camps.

Becoming a teacher

My civil engineering career having been cut short, I was invited to teach at a farming project run by a man who had once commanded 300 guerilla independence fighters. After serving seven years in jail, he was released. On a farm, he set up a training program for about 30 youngsters too poor to afford a formal education.

For several months I taught basic elementary subjects to these boys. I developed a taste for teaching. At the same time, I learned much about the independence movement from this man, who often held my attention until late into the night with his stories. I learned from him that the struggle for human liberation is not all heroic and glorious. Reality is far more ambiguous than romantic visions or ideology would have us believe.

Convinced now that I should take up teaching as a career, I enrolled in studies to obtain a teacher's license. The course normally took a year to complete. But in early 1945, as World War II reached its climax in Asia, all fields were feeling shortages. Professional schools were being pushed to graduate more people, more rapidly. As a result, my study time was cut to six months.

By the summer of 1945, I returned home to my parents in Yong Jung, ready to begin teaching primary school.

Summoned by the police

Several days after my return, I received a letter summoning me immediately to the police station. My heart sank. This could mean only one thing, I thought. My options were very limited. If I did go, I felt sure I would be drafted for military service. If I did not go, there would be inquiries. I would be a fugitive. Perhaps they would interrogate my father.

I was tempted to complain to God. I felt let down and forsaken, after having been such a good Christian. But when I closed my eyes to pray that night, I realized that I had already been spared for more than two years, while other young men were lost in battle. I felt ashamed and resolved to face whatever needed to be faced the next day.

At the police station, instead of handing me my papers and my orders, the man behind the desk asked me where I had been for the past two years.

The question took me by surprise. The Japanese, as I knew from experience, were meticulous record-keepers. All information about my life should be contained in my papers. The police kept a dossier on every man, woman and youth. Whenever I moved to a new location for more than three months, my dossier would be transferred to the police station of the new locality.

If they did not know where I had been for the past years, they might draw the wrong conclusions, I feared. I asked the policeman why he put such a question to me. The information should be in my records, I told him.

In a somewhat annoyed tone he responded, "That is precisely the point. We are unable to locate your records!"

I had to give them details of all my movements, all the cities and towns I had been in, all my jobs, for the previous two years. They said they would investigate. In early August, I stood before them again. The records had been located. The police in one of the towns had put them in the wrong filing cabinet, where they had gathered dust. The mystery of my exemption from the draft had finally been solved.

But the war was still raging. I was given strict orders not to go anywhere. In two days my dossier would arrive from the other city. Then I could be called up for military service at any time.

On that very day, August 6, 1945, an atomic bomb devastated Hiroshima. Three days later, Nagasaki suffered the same fate. On August 8, Soviet troops invaded Manchuria, encountering little resistance. A week later, Emperor Hirohito broadcast his surrender decision to the Japanese people. The war was over!

I realized then that God had indeed spared my life. I fell on my knees to give thanks, and as I had promised I dedicated my life to God.

When the author (centre) re-visited Manchuria, in 1986, at the invitation of the Chinese authorities, he found the church he had once attended in Yong Jung. Though the building was no longer used as a church, there were still Christians worshipping in the town.

Flight into Korea

Koreans and Chinese equated the defeat of Japan with their own liberation. Political detainees came out of jails; prisoners of war were released from detention camps; exiles began returning home. Thousands of Koreans headed for their homeland. Country roads and highways were jammed with people moving in every direction.

For the Japanese and their collaborators, this was a time of humiliation and terror. Anger had built up for so many years that a spirit of revenge swept through the country. Murder and retaliation were common. Japanese soldiers and policemen preferred to surrender as prisoners of war rather than to risk mob lynchings.

Returning home from another town during those days, I spotted a figure by the side of the road, his head turned away, his shoulders hunched, afraid to be recognized. But even if he had worn a disguise I would have known him. He was the interrogator, the traitor who had tortured my friends and me for two weeks back in high school, for the "crime" of studying our own—and his own—native language.

My immediate reaction was to find a large rock and beat it on his head.

A short distance away, a group of people rested with sacks and baskets. If I told them who this man was, they would gladly help me dispatch him. I felt a supreme elation. God had spared me from military service, and God had delivered my enemy into my hands. I remembered the Old Testament stories where the enemies of Israel were ruthlessly slaughtered.

But I hesitated. I could not do it. I did not like the hot anger that flooded me. I wondered what Jesus might do, in a similar circumstance, and immediately realized he would not even have contemplated such vengeance. He gave his own life for the very people who crucified him, asking God to forgive them even as he hung on the cross. It was this God of the weak, of the poor, of the sick and downtrodden, to whom I had surrendered my life, not the God of power and retribution.

The man noticed someone on the road behind him. He glanced fearfully over his shoulder, and recognized me too. He cringed and trembled. I would have liked to tell him I forgave him, as Jesus had done, but I did not have Jesus' strength. The way he cowered before me raised my anger once more. He was a despicable, pitiful man—letting him live was my best revenge.

I told him that I could readily have killed him, but that I would not do it. This was a time for Koreans to celebrate liberation and freedom; these belonged to *all* Koreans, even those who did not deserve it. I thrust out my hand, and told him that I wished to shake hands for Korea's future.

He was overcome with emotion and bowed to me repeatedly, thanking me. I left him there by the side of the road, grateful that I had not done something stupid. Nevertheless, in a way I had not expected, I had satisfied my desire for vengeance.

I began to understand that the Christian precepts of forgiveness and benevolence are not simply ideals for self-improvement. They have practical significance as well. Anger and revenge are self-destructive and perpetuate violence. Overcoming that violence within ourselves brings a healing power into society. Making peace is much more difficult than making war. Yet it is also infinitely more productive.

Under Soviet rule

At the end of the war, the USA occupied Japan and Korea south of the 38th parallel; the USSR did the same for Manchuria and northern Korea.

Forgetting that it was the Japanese whom they had defeated, not the local inhabitants, the Soviet troops behaved like conquerors. Raping and looting, they swept like bandits from town to town. Women hid from them; men tried to defend their property. The Soviet soldiers raided factories and shipped machinery back to Russia. They entered private homes and took anything that pleased them.

History had caught up with us again. We had escaped from Soviet communism by fleeing from Siberia into China when I was only seven years old. Now, 14 years later, we found ourselves once more under the authority of communist troops.

Because my father spoke fluent Russian from our time in Siberia, he was often called to interpret, or to mediate in disputes. I witnessed one such encounter. The son of a neighboring family came running one day, begging my father to hurry to their house. I ran along as well. When we arrived there, we saw broken dishes and scattered furniture. Three obviously inebriated soldiers were keeping family and neighbors at bay, boisterously shouting and laughing, while two others had cornered a young woman and were about to assault her.

I can still see my father, facing these battle-worn soldiers, speaking quietly to them in the Russian language. "You are our friends," he said to them. "You have liberated our country. We Koreans like you. We are your neighbors."

I will never forget the change that came over those soldiers when they heard their own language spoken. They stood in amazed silence. In that brief moment, they changed from carousing animals into humans. They calmed down and began conversing with my father, asking him where he had learned to speak Russian, telling him where they had come from.

My father suggested to the family that they offer some small gifts to the soldiers as souvenirs. The soldiers became calm, pensive. They shook hands, apologized, and went their way.

From that day on, I have respected the immense power of one's own native language. Our language identifies us with a community, gives us self-respect, makes us human. I suddenly realized the logic, as well as the folly, of the Japanese prohibition of the Korean language. It was meant to rob us of our identity as a people, and thus to make us pliable for their designs. Instead, it united us in our determination to resist.

I had no need to be convinced, when I eventually came to Canada, that language is crucial to Canada's identity. I could understand the importance of a bilingual nation.

But precisely because of this, I am also a defender of all language rights— from Canada's Native peoples to Canada's most recent immigrants. It makes me a staunch defender of multiculturalism in Canada as a whole, and in The United Church of Canada in particular.

Under surveillance

I taught primary school throughout the fall of that year. My excitement about prospects of independence for Korea grew. A number of my friends, including Kang Won-Yong and his family, had already returned there.

In school I filled the children's heads with patriotic ideas. The future looked so bright that I neglected to pay attention to the clouds already forming on the horizon. In October 1945, the USA and the USSR, occupying the two parts of Korea, announced that Korea would not become independent after all.

In the territories occupied by the Soviet Union, including Manchuria where I was living, Stalinist law and order began to be felt. In schools, separation of education and religion was rigidly enforced. I was told politely but firmly that as a teacher I could *attend* religious worship, but I should not *participate* in any other church activities.

I decided to ignore the order. We had entered the busy Advent season, and I had direct responsibility for many functions planned at the church. As superintendent of Sunday school, I could hardly take a back seat.

Friends began to warn me that I was under surveillance. No matter, I thought, I had given my life to God, and I wasn't about to miss the excitement of a marvelous Christmas season, our first truly "free" Christmas since the defeat of the Japanese oppressors!

Christmas day came. The church was filled with people. We had a long, triumphant service. The children put on a heart-warming Christmas pageant. Mary and Joseph and the angels and shepherds and wise men were all proud Koreans with Korean names. The choir sang anthems in a Korean language that never sounded so beautiful. The pastor's sermon expressed the joy of all of us at the rich blessings the Lord had provided for us. Our prayers of thanks rang out so loudly, the building seemed to tremble.

Near the end of the service, an elder approached me quietly. He warned me that there were two men standing in the cold at the front gate of the church. They had asked for me. They were unwilling to enter the church and make a spectacle of my arrest, so they were waiting for me to leave. He suggested I take an alternate route home.

With the congregation's dispersal providing a diversion at the front of the church, I slipped out the back. Instead of returning home, I went to the house of a friend. I asked him to go to my house and check what was happening. He returned with the news I had feared. The two men were now at my house, obviously waiting for me.

I remained with my friend that night. The mysterious men waited for me right through the night.

Escape to Korea

I decided to leave town until things cooled down. I knew I would lose my teaching job. But that was better than being arrested, I thought. I felt sure that my case was not so important that they would continue to look for me for very long. I asked my friend to visit my parents the next day, and to inform them that I would be gone for a little while. I would come back soon.

Early the next morning, in biting cold weather, I jumped on the back of a truck headed towards Korea. I knew that Kang Won-Yong had moved to the northern part of Korea, and decided to try to find him.

To keep warm as the truck lurched along the bumpy road, I huddled in a corner. I clutched my Bible, my only possession apart from the clothes I had worn to church, and wondered what it would be like to live in my homeland Korea for the very first time.

I had no idea, as we crossed into Korea, that I would never see my father, my mother, my sisters or my younger brothers again.

A refugee once more

With little information, but a lot of walking, hitch-hiking and asking directions, I managed to find the Kang Won-Yong family in North Korea. But Won-Yong had already gone south, to Seoul. He was active politically, and Seoul was the place for non-communist nationalists to be at this time.

During this period, some two million Koreans flooded into southern Korea—from China, from Japan, and from the north. This migration was fueled by fears of communism, and by the inability of the superpowers to agree on Korea's future. The US wanted to ensure that Korea remained within the Western camp, as a bastion of its "containment of communism" doctrine. The USSR wanted to ensure that any Korean government would include its communist protegés, to guarantee a friendly buffer state on its eastern flank.

In migrating south, men usually went ahead to try to establish themselves in jobs and housing before bringing their families to join them. Practically everyone believed that Korea would soon be unified again. Few realized how quickly the situation would deteriorate; no one predicted international war would soon break out on Korean soil.

I was one of those naïve ones. I sent word to my parents, through a friend, that I planned to go on to Seoul for further education. But I would return to Manchuria during the summer, I promised.

Kang Won-Yong, hearing of my plans, sent me a message to bring his family to Seoul. So after the spring thaw, Won-Yong's wife and two daughters made the journey south with me.

We approached the border in early March, 1946. Soviet troops were guarding the bridge across the Imjin River. We knew we would not be permitted to cross, so we returned to the nearest town.

As always, wherever there is a need, someone will find a way to profit from it. For a price, we could make arrangements to cross the border. The deal cost us the rest of our money—just as it had cost my parents, leaving Siberia— but with some luck, we would soon be in Seoul.

The "arrangements" proved effective. The guard at the bridge had obviously been bribed. As we approached, he turned his attention away from the bridge, apparently engrossed in the spring scenery. We crossed without incident.

Safe passages such as ours diminished with time. A year later, people had to risk their lives crossing the same river in boats at night. Many were shot, or caught and taken back.

I was by no means confident, as I crossed into the southern half of Korea, that this was where I wanted to go. Like my country, I was not in control. But I had neither the conviction nor the courage to swim against the current.

And so, rootless and drifting, I arrived in Seoul.

A refugee in my own homeland

Continuing my education was impossible without money. I looked for work, but jobs were short. Japanese exploitation had left Korea in shambles. The military government which the Americans had set up was neither competent to reorganize the economy, nor ready to trust Koreans to do it themselves.

The south had always been mainly agricultural. Heavy industry was mainly in the north, where munitions factories supplied Japanese troops in Manchuria and China. The few factories in the south stood idle. Although farmers pressed for the removal of the Japanese tenant system, the Americans hesitated. They saw the peasants as communist-inspired. Blinded by their anti-communism, the Americans had, in fact, aligned themselves with the formerly pro-Japanese landowners and wealthy people.

To remedy drastic shortages, the USA began importing food and clothing. But these imports undermined our own small domestic enterprises. Japanese mines and factories, expropriated by the military government, were redistributed to pro-American political parties. Out of these parties came the personalities who have ruled South Korean business and politics ever since.

Of course, I was unaware of all this. All I knew was that jobs were impossible to find. I lived from hand to mouth for almost a year, doing odd jobs for people and selling goods door-to-door. Transport and distribution were so poor that I could make money by walking to rural areas, buying rice and bringing it back into the city to sell.

I finally found a steady job in an orphanage. In the daytime, I was teacher to about 130 boys and girls; in the evening I became a surrogate father to 30 of them. Meanwhile, I kept fretting over my promise to God.

Deep in my heart, I suspected that my promise to offer myself to God meant going into the ordained ministry. But for some reason I hesitated. The aftermath of the war, the misery of poverty, the division and insecurity of Korea, and not least, my separation from my family, which had now lasted for over a year with no end in sight—all these had become burdens my immaturity found hard to bear.

My pious, fundamentalist, charismatic Christian education had not prepared me for such heaviness of soul. My faith hit rock bottom. At one point, I consulted a friend, a brilliant young minister whom I had met in Manchuria. I told him that I was thinking of studying for the ministry. He looked at me sideways and said, "Do you have to do that?"

I told him that I had made a promise to offer myself to God.

He replied gently, "Don't be foolish. The ministry is not the only way you can serve God."

A new vision

Then I met Kim Chai-Choon. At that time he was Principal of Chosun Theological Seminary in Seoul. Even back in Manchuria I had heard about him. He had taught Bible and English at my high school before I started there.

The Rev. Kim Chai-Choon was pastor of Kyongdong Presbyterian Church, which I joined when I arrived in Seoul. My friend Kang Won-Yong, a co-founder of that church, was an elder and his assistant. I became steward, in charge of Sunday school. Many of that church's young people, myself included, became leaders in the Korean Student Christian Federation, which strongly opposed the policies first of the military government and then the Syngman Rhee regime.

Pastor Kim Chai-Choon opened up totally different ways to think about Christianity. This man was not a hero-type. He was quiet, even shy. But once he began to speak, once he mounted the pulpit and began to preach, his energy almost swallowed me. He spoke simply, with great sincerity, but I came to be nourished by the power which emanated from his every word.

If only for the sake of studying under this man, if only to glean as much as I could of his wisdom, I decided that studying theology was, after all, what I should be doing.

Studies towards ordination

So I began theological studies in April 1947. I continued those studies during the Korean war, when the seminary itself became fugitive and had to move south to Pusan. Finally, after the war, with the seminary re-established in Seoul, I returned for graduate studies and obtained my Master of Theology Degree in 1956.

My formative influence, without doubt, was Kim Chai-Choon. The way he taught theology healed the tensions between personal spirituality and social conscience that had been tearing me apart. Not that these tensions have been eliminated. Even today they affect me. But Kim Chai-Choon's theology gave me perspectives to analyze and accept them and to deal with them.

Christianity had originally come as a form of escape for me. I had a lot of anger towards society. I felt helpless, and that in turn led to more anger, which built up within me like a poison. The church I attended gave me a community to belong to, and a retreat from reality. It helped to get rid of some of the poison inside. I experienced healing, as I realized much later. Had I not been able to rid myself of that poison, I could well have become mentally ill.

Yet all the same, the church where I came to know the power of the Holy Spirit also taught me a negative attitude towards the world. As a secure refuge, the church made the real world seem that much more demonic, that much more poisonous. Yet somehow, God provided me with a basic moral outrage which refused to allow me to retreat completely from human concerns, from social concerns, from concerns for my people.

Though I couldn't articulate it then, I was searching for an alternate way to be Christian. I wanted to keep the authenticity of my original Christian experience, but I wanted also to be fully a part of the real world.

Through Kim Chai-Choon's Old Testament classes I learned new ways of looking at the prophets. Through him, I understood more fully what had always attracted me about Moses. My former teachers had portrayed him only as a miracle performer. Now I came to appreciate Moses' love for his own people, and the struggle of the children of Israel for liberation. Suddenly I became aware of the deeply political character of the Bible.

Kim Chai-Choon knew contemporary Western theologians such as Karl Barth, Emil Brunner, Reinhold Niebuhr. But he neither copied their ideas nor gave us endless quotations. He had a talent for absorbing other people's theologies and coming out with his own. We found it easy to relate to his teaching. Somehow it was Christianity within the unique Korean experience.

On being introduced to this liberating Christianity, my first reaction was anger. I felt misled, even betrayed, by those who had previously engulfed me in a pious and static spirituality. Then I began to feel sorry for Christians who limit the Christ to being their own personal savior in their own private domain. I could see certain Christians around me withdrawing more and more from the world, filled with negative attitudes. I was aware of them, because in many ways I myself was still one of them.

In studying the life of Jesus, I found a person who did not deny or withdraw. He constantly led his disciples back to the world, down from the mountain, into the sinfulness and corruption of Jerusalem. His last commandment to all of us was to "go out into the world and preach the Gospel." To this Jesus I now turned.

A wanderer as model for my life

One of my favorite literary figures in those days was the 19th century poet Kim Sakkat, who had traveled the country begging like a vagabond while tirelessly preaching against false pride and hypocrisy. Hundreds of poems and stories are attributed to this anti-establishment wanderer. His humor, wisdom and way of life made a strong impression on me. This is how I imagined the Old Testament prophets to have lived. Wasn't even Jesus like this, challenging the Pharisees, the powers and principalities, without a place to lay his head?

At one point, I almost followed in the footsteps of Kim Sakkat. I was acquainted with a man who lived outside of Seoul, in a cave which the Japanese had once used as a munitions dump. After receiving a university education in Tokyo, this man had returned to Korea, but became so disgusted by political and social developments that he became a kind of hermit anarchist.

I more or less became his disciple. Almost every day I visited him. We sat in his cave, engaging in endless philosophical and political discussions about life, purpose and the shape of Korea. Sometimes I joined him when he went out begging for food in the city streets. I felt that I should not become committed to any earthly institution. I should be a totally free person, able to say what I liked, and then to move on. I rather enjoyed the idea of being a voice crying in the wilderness.

But after a while, something within would begin to bug me again. "How can you forget the world?" it demanded. "How can you criticize the lack of responsibility in others when you do not take any responsibility yourself? Should you not be there, playing your part, however inadequate?"

Then I would come back into society to try again, like a pendulum. Had the Korean war not interfered, I do not know which way of life I would have finally chosen. My wandering in the wilderness was just another aspect of my education. At the time, I didn't know that, but God knew.

When he heard that I had been elected Moderator of The United Church of Canada, Rev. Park Hyung-Kyu, a friend who knew my past life well, teased me: "How can that Canadian church choose a Korean beggar as its leader?" He was quite right in his description of me. In some ways I have not changed at all. I am not one who enjoys titles and fancy words. I wear them poorly. They do not fit the country boy from Siberia.

The tensions grow

The northern part of Korea became the Democratic People's Republic , led by Kim Il-Sung, who had spent the war years in the Soviet Union. The southern part became the Republic of Korea, under Syngman Rhee, who had spent the war years in the USA.

Syngman Rhee ruled with an iron hand. Any students originating in the north were suspect. Those who proved themselves avidly anti-communist were recruited to hunt down those considered to have leftist leanings.

For a while I was supervising minister, under the United Church of Canada Mission Board, at two dormitories for students from the north. It was not uncommon for students to be kidnapped from this residence, and lynched somewhere. Often their bodies could not be located; the police pretended to know nothing.

Syngman Rhee had a knack for manipulating the anti-communism of conservative church people. When the government wanted to increase military aid from the USA, a huge Christian demonstration was organized to support that appeal. Our own church was against an arms race in Korea, and particularly against Christians demanding military aid and weapons. Because we boycotted that demonstration, our church was threatened with arson.

In 1949, the communist People's Republic of China was founded. Again I wondered what had happened to my family. For four years, I had heard nothing from them. Now there was no way for me to communicate with them—even to know if they were still in China or had moved to North Korea. Many of us had a high commitment to re-unification; giving up on it meant giving up any hope of ever seeing our parents and loved ones again.

I graduated from Seminary in April 1950 and was appointed to a small parish half an hour's drive north of Seoul. The people were very poor, with neither telephones nor radios. I enjoyed the quiet of the countryside. It was refreshing after the hectic city life in Seoul.

On a rainy Sunday morning, June 25, 1950, we held our church service at 11:00 as usual. The congregation went home. About mid-afternoon, someone told us that the Northern armies had invaded the South and were heading our way.

Everything seemed so peaceful. But at 4:00 o'clock that morning, an estimated 90,000 North Korean troops, including 150 heavy tanks, had crossed the 38th parallel and begun the Korean War.

A nation of refugees

By the time I got up the next day, a stream of people was moving south on the road. By the time I had washed and had some breakfast, the stream had enlarged to hundreds and thousands. At the same time, members of the Korean army moved in the opposite direction in jeeps and trucks and on foot. I saw no tanks or heavy equipment.

The refugees told us they were fleeing the front lines, hoping to seek refuge in the capital. The police and military advised us to remain where we were. "There is nothing to fear," they said.

By the afternoon, we could hear the sound of mortar fire in the distance. North Korean planes flew above us towards Seoul.

I had a restless sleep. The noise of gunfire continued through the night; I had a distinct impression that it was coming closer. When I got up on Tuesday, June 27, I decided there was really no use in staying in this place any longer. I locked up dutifully, though uselessly, and caught a train to

Seoul. The train was crammed, but I managed to squeeze in. On the way, a North Korean airplane strafed us.

In Seoul, an ocean of people were all leaving the city, carrying whatever belongings they could. I seemed to be the only person going against the stream, into the city. I went to Kyongdong Presbyterian church, to find my friends. There was no one there. Everyone had already left. People advised me to leave while it was still possible to cross the Han river.

By that afternoon, I was at the river, but the four bridges were hopelessly packed with military vehicles going one way and crowds of refugees going the other. Hardly anything moved. I joined the thousands at the bank of the river, waiting for a place on one of the few boats. Throughout the day, I was told, the voice of President Syngman Rhee came over the radio, urging people to remain calm and not to leave the city. Later, we discovered that he and his family had left the city the day before.

I looked around at women carrying enormous bundles of clothes wrapped in sheets, while holding little crying children. Infants were being carried like luggage; old men and women bent from long years of hard labor in the rice fields waited. Many men used the traditional Korean wooden back-pack frames to carry burdens that included everything from pots and pans to tools and food, occasionally with a child sitting on top of the whole load.

At about 2:00 in the morning, we were wakened by an enormous explosion. Later, word reached us that the army had blown up the bridges to delay the further advance of Northern armies. In exploding one bridge, the rumors raced through the crowd, they had killed hundreds of refugees and even a truckload of soldiers who were still on it.

It was pouring rain, with dawn just starting the morning of Wednesday June 28, when I got near a boat. I helped a family lift their small children aboard, then found a place for myself. That evening, the capital fell to the invaders.

Drifting south

Lacking any other means of transportation, I walked the whole night to Suwon, the first large city south of Seoul. Repeatedly I was stopped and questioned by police. The fact that I was alone, young and empty-handed, made me both visible and suspect. They thought I must be either an escaped prisoner or a spy.

Others seemed to envy the fact that I carried no belongings, had no children to look after. But I would gladly have shared the necessary responsibilities and difficulties, if only I could enjoy the comfort of a companion.

Soldiers were already withdrawing from the front, passing by in trucks carrying the wounded. They seemed ashamed to look people in the eye. Defeat was written on their faces.

Suwon was jammed with military. I was advised to leave immediately; this was expected to be the next major battle against the North.

Dead tired from having walked all night, I decided to try the railway station. I was in luck. There was a train in the station. Tickets were not required. The train, the longest I had ever seen, was made up mostly of freight cars, packed so tightly with human cargo that not an inch remained into which I could squeeze. Even on the roofs, every available space was taken up with people and their belongings.

The train began to pull out of the station. Without thinking, I ran to the nearest car, climbed onto the external ladder and simply hung on. As the train picked up speed and the wind blew against my face, the fatigue of two nights without sleep washed over me. My eyes closed. I snapped to attention just as my grip began to loosen. If I fell asleep, I would fall under the wheels of the train.

At the next station I jumped off and searched desperately until I found some pieces of rope. Using these, I tied myself to the ladder. In this awkward but safer position, I continued south. Behind me, I heard sounds of bombardment, as Suwon came under attack.

Rejecting the truth

I stood in the crowd at Chonan, tired, hungry, and without any conviction. It was the most negative experience I'd had in my life. I was angry at the government, which had cheated the people out of its liberation. I was angry at the Northerners for inflicting pain and suffering on their own people. And I suppose I was angry at myself for drifting once more like flotsam on the tide, without direction, without purpose.

Then as I stood there, lost and confused, I heard my name called. I turned but couldn't recognize any of the thousands of faces around me.

"Lee Sang-Chul, older brother," the voice repeated directly behind me. It was Yang Jun-Chul, a young member of Kyongdong Presbyterian Church, whom I had always treated as a brother. We hugged each other and wept for joy.

When he discovered that I had no place to go, Jun-Chul invited me to come with him to his mother in Chungju, a city to the east. A train took us several stations further. Then we managed to climb on the back of a truck.

Numerous times we were stopped at roadblocks. Everybody had to get down to identify themselves.

At the first roadblock, Jun-Chul and I told the policeman that we had come from Seoul. He asked us what had happened there. Innocently, we reported that the capital was already occupied by North Korean troops. Before I could react, I received a vicious kick to my stomach. The policeman began to beat us, shouting that we were liars and communist spies.

My immediate reaction was reckless anger. Then the policeman drew his revolver and aimed it at us.

"I could kill you," he threatened. "But I will let you go if you promise never to repeat the lies you just told me. Seoul is in our hands, and North Korean troops are well within their territory."

After we agreed to watch our tongues, he allowed us to board the truck again. A dozen checkpoints later we arrived in Chungju, having learned the value of ignorance.

For two weeks I stayed with Yang Jun-Chul's mother. At church on Sunday I encountered two women I had known in Manchuria. The elder one was a "Bible woman," a lay minister. She had served a small congregation close to the 38th parallel, now displaced by the war. She was accompanied by a young kindergarten teacher who had been a pupil of mine when I taught primary school in Manchuria. The young woman was taking care of her parish minister's two little children. The minister and his wife had gone to Seoul when the war broke out. No one had heard from them since.

After two weeks, the war neared again. Citizens of Chungju were advised to move south. The Bible woman said to me, "You are single, you have no belongings. We are two women with two girls but no man to help us. Why don't you accompany us on our flight as 'head of the family'?"

For the first time since my flight began, I was carrying luggage on my back and holding the hands of little girls. We walked from Chungju to Taejon, staying in a church overnight. But the United Nations troops, setting up a defence line at Taejon, urged us to continue southward.

To get a train to Pusan, we had a three hour walk. It was already late in the afternoon. When the sun went down, we found ourselves in the country-side, far from any city or town. In a nearby farmyard, we discovered some hay stacks. The farmer gave us permission to sleep in the hay. After we got settled, however, a group of young boys surrounded us and began to threaten us, calling us communists and spies.

I became angry. "We have our homes, just as you do," I yelled, "but we lost them because of the war. Even you do not know how long you can keep your homes. This is a critical time for Korea. We must all help each other. If you mistreat refugees like us, then you must yourselves be in sympathy with the invaders." We were finally left in peace under the hay.

We managed to get onto a train to Taegu, where a minister friend provided shelter for us in a corner of his church, already filled with refugees. But in Taegu, I lost my little family. They no longer needed me. The parents of the two children were found in Taegu. The kindergarten teacher found her older sister. And the Bible woman told me not to worry about her; she had been independent her whole life long.

No place to die

So I was alone again. I began to brood. The war would soon catch up with us. Taegu was the last possible line of defence. I began thinking about dying.

Whenever I thought about the end of my life, I always worried about where I should lay my body. Perhaps this is the psychological problem of a homeless man. The Korean word "kohyang" carries more emotion than its English equivalent, "home town." In Korean custom, the first time you meet someone, you ask: "Where is your kohyang?" But I never had a kohyang.

So I had no place to die.

Finally I realized that if the end were to come, I would prefer to die with friends. One of these was the Rev. Kang Sung-Kap, a brilliant scholar who served a church in the small town of Jingyoung, just north of Pusan. He had founded a high school for peasant children who had no money for higher education. Hanul High School's simple classrooms were built entirely by the students themselves, under his supervision.

Kang Sung-Kap could have escaped the war. He had an invitation from Princeton Seminary to do graduate studies with a full scholarship. In fact, he had obtained his passport and visas when the students, their parents, and the entire community of farmers, pleaded with him not to go. If he left, they told him, the school would be closed; their children would forfeit the chance of an education. Kang cancelled his scholarship.

In a letter to the Rev. Kang, I offered my services for whatever I might do around the school. "Come right away," he cabled in reply.

I told him that I feared this war was headed for disaster. "I have no place on this earth to go," I told him. "I would like to die in your town."

Kang laughed. "Don't worry," he said. "You're not going to die yet."

His easy confidence humbled and puzzled me. How could he be so sure? And yet he was right. There was really no reason why I was in any more danger than any other Korean. Instead of sinking into gloom, I should have realized that his own position was far more vulnerable than mine. Yet he had much more faith.

At his home in Jingyoung, we ate a simple dinner of rice and kimchi. There was not much food in those days. Yet it seemed like a feast to me.

Kang had a close friend, a Mr. Chae, the local correspondent of the national newspaper *Dong-A Ilbo*. Both men were intensely disliked by local officials. Because the people trusted Kang, they told him the truth about the politicians; through this relationship, Chae exposed all kinds of local corruption in his newspaper.

Several weeks later, Kang went to visit his brother. The next morning, his brother told us that the police had arrested Kang late the previous evening. Kang's friend Chae had also disappeared.

A few days later, we were summoned to identify a body washed up on the bank of the river. The body had already begun to decompose. It was Kang. We could see bullet wounds in several places.

The policemen ordered us to bury the body on the riverside, right where it was found. No funeral, no publicity, no inquiry. When we asked about Mr. Chae, we were warned not to ask questions, nor to say anything to anyone about this incident.

Propaganda warfare

I had escaped actual combat by coming to the only part of the country, later called the "Pusan perimeter," that was never overrun by the North. But the death of Rev. Kang showed clearly that I had not escaped the war.

As the war continued, we heard more and more reports of indiscriminate killings of civilians, massacres of men, women and children, pillaging of towns and cities, rape, torture and other atrocities. I still cannot comprehend how cruel my people could be. It was as if we had internalized all the hatred left over from the Japanese oppression and from World War II, and had taken it out against ourselves.

Searching for a job in Pusan, I heard of an opening for translators from English to Korean. Although the English I had learned in seminary was elementary, few Koreans knew any English at all in those days. I was hired by the Cultural Information Office of the USA, which, I soon suspected, was actually a front for the Central Intelligence Agency.

My job, it turned out, was to translate American propaganda literature into Korean. I had to use my dictionary for every other word. Still, it was a good exercise for me, and my English improved. Although I can boast that my translations were printed in hundreds of thousands, I will never know how many readers I actually had, or their opinion of my work. The leaflets containing my translations were dropped from planes behind enemy lines.

Apart from being a salaried man now, there was another benefit. This job was considered so important that it saved me from military service.

None of us in the Pusan area realized how international the war had become. Sixteen countries, including Canada, responded to the United Nations call to help the USA repel the North Koreans. On September 15, General MacArthur landed in Inchon, the seaport near Seoul, and began to push back the Northern army. By mid-November, they had succeeded not only in re-taking the South, but the North as well, right up to the Yalu River.

A survivor returns

One evening, as we sat and relaxed after supper, we heard a knock. When I opened the door, I stepped back, speechless. In the doorway stood a ghost—Mr. Chae, the journalist who was supposed to have died with Rev. Kang Sung-Kap.

Chae, amused at our alarm, broke the silence. He entered the room, favoring his leg, and asked for something to drink. We served him tea while he told us what had happened to him.

Local politicians and the police chief had been plotting for some time to rid themselves of their two nuisances, Kang and Chae, he said. One day, a military recruiting officer came to town. As they wined and dined the officer in Korean style, with young ladies in attendance, the military man boasted more and more about the number of communists he had already killed.

The hosts seized their chance. They told the drunken man of two communists, in this very town, who had defied every effort to be caught. The military officer, suggesting that communists did not deserve the due process of law, immediately offered to rectify the situation.

Kang and Chae were seized and taken to the river. They were given a chance to say some last words. Chae defiantly told them he had nothing to say. Kang knelt and prayed. He prayed for his own soul, for Chae, and for his executioners, asking God to forgive them, as they didn't know what they were doing.

Then the two men were pushed into the river. The assembled police and military men emptied their revolvers at them. Chae, however, had been a champion swimmer in his younger days, and was still in excellent shape. As soon as he hit the water, he submerged and swam upstream, while the assassins aimed their shots downstream. Even so, he was hit twice, once in the shoulder and once in the leg. He managed to hide at the edge of the river until the police left. For several months, he hid in the mountains.

He asked us to report this matter, to have the killers prosecuted. Since it appeared at that time that the war would soon be won, the authorities were eager to demonstrate their responsible attitudes. Fourteen town officials were arrested and charged; two were sentenced to death for Kang's murder.

Trying to trace my family

In our euphoria as the Northern armies retreated, we imagined a speedy re-unification of our country. I began to dream of meeting my family again.

Then China intervened. Though they had poor equipment, they had overwhelming numbers. They pushed the UN forces back and re-took Seoul by January 1951. By March and April, the USA and its allies, using the latest military technology and blanket bombing the north, pushed the battle lines back to the 38th parallel again.

Truce talks began that June. For two more years, the conflict continued, though no major territory was again taken by either side.

An armistice was signed on July 27, 1953, but true peace has never been concluded. In 1989, 36 years later, Korea is still officially at war. We will probably never know how many people actually died in Korea in those three years. Estimates indicate that over 3 million Koreans, over 1.5 million Chinese and some 370,000 UN troops (including 516 Canadians) died during this brief war. Millions more were wounded and crippled for life. The number of refugees produced by this conflict will never be counted. The number of separated Korean family members is estimated to be 10 million.

Over the years, I have questioned anyone who came from the North about my family. The only reference came third hand. A friend of mine had met a woman refugee from the North who was a school friend of my brother's wife. Apparently my brother's wife told this woman that her husband had an older brother in Seoul (myself). Unfortunately, my brother was in military service, so they had to await his return before attempting to escape to the south. My brother's wife was pregnant at the time.

That is the only information I have about my family to this day.

Settling down

Given my negative, pessimistic attitudes, especially during the harshness of war, I am still surprised that I ever got married.

The problem was not a lack of candidates. In Korea, close friends customarily try to find an appropriate match. For years, they suggested all kinds of names to me. The problem was my attitude towards marriage. I felt that I should not make any woman miserable.

My experience of family life was a gloomy one. I could see only visions of poverty: working tirelessly just to make ends meet, bringing children into this valley of tears without the means to raise and educate them. It had a lot to do with my own experience. But I also saw no chance of improvement in our country's situation, nor any bright prospects for my own future. In my eyes, it would be unfair for me to propose marriage to any woman, and particularly any woman I cared for.

As a result, I kept all relationships at arms-length. Except for one woman, Kim Shin-Jah, the daughter of seminary principal Kim Chai-Choon. I had known her for a long time. She attended the same church as I did. She graduated from Chosun Theological Seminary a year prior to me. I had a lot of respect for her and enjoyed her company.

This feeling seems to have been mutual, though we never expressed it to each other. I certainly never considered it possible for me—a "Korean beggar," as Park Hyung-Ku put it many years later—to have any chance of marrying that great man's daughter. I thought I was safe!

Besides, many other young men were making eyes at Shin-Jah. Professor Kim could not have been unaware of this. In the Confucian tradition (which never really leaves you, though your religion may change), an important man such as Kim Chai-Choon would consider a variety of options for linking families through marriage. Even my match-making friends never considered suggesting this match to me.

I don't remember exactly how it happened. But one morning I woke up and realized that, the day before, Shin-Jah and I had agreed to get married. I was terrified. How were we going to break this news to her father?

We decided to ask Kang Won-Yong to be our go-between. As he later reported, Shin-Jah's father was quite taken aback. "Who is this Lee Sang-Chul?" he demanded. Of course, he knew me as a student. But he didn't know me as a prospective son-in-law. He didn't know my family background, because I had none. I had no roots, no family tree.

This was going to be even more difficult than I thought. "How are we going to speak to your father?" I asked Shin-Jah, knowing her to be a shy and obedient daughter. I soon discovered that this woman could also be very determined and courageous. "Don't worry about it," she told me calmly, "I will tell my father."

Her father, after letting the proposal sink in, simply said to her—as my parents had said about my conversion to Christianity—"You are old enough to make your own decisions about your life."

A national social event

In Korean custom, the groom's family makes all the arrangements. Since I was all by myself, I wanted to have a very small ceremony, involving only Shin-Jah's immediate family and our closest friends.

My future father-in-law would have none of this. His daughter must be married in style! Since my family could not look after the necessary arrangements, he took it upon himself to organize the event.

I discovered him to be a most generous, charitable person. But I watched helplessly as wedding plans expanded into a major national social event. When he proposed that the nation's vice-president, Mr. Ham Tae-Young, pronounce the benediction, I knew I had lost control once more, this time of what was supposedly the most important ceremony of my life.

I had always been allergic to pomp and formality, but this went far beyond my expectations. In vain I tried to object, but confronted with the

Above: the wedding party.
Below: the bride and groom.

power of my bride's father, any objections sounded silly, even to me. Since the vice-president was a good friend of my father-in-law, and a member of our church, I was told it would be an affront not to invite him. And if he was invited, he had to be given a prominent role. Reluctantly, I gave in.

It was a bright, beautiful spring day—a perfect day for a wedding, as my wife has always reminded me. With freshness in the air and cherry blossoms to add color to the scene on April 8, 1953, it was difficult to imagine that war still raged somewhere to the north of us.

In the barracks which served as the seminary auditorium, one of my professors performed the ceremony. Since no member of my family could be present to fulfill the traditional duty of responding with thanks and welcome, Kang Won-Yong performed this function. Some 200 guests attended the wedding banquet. Thankfully, the feast itself was a modest one, since war conditions still prevailed. It was also more appropriate to my parents' social status, and to my state of mind.

The pain every Korean knows

The evening of a Korean wedding is usually spent at home with one's closest friends. As my mother-in-law brought more food and rice wine, we began to reminisce about those who could not share this moment with us—those from whom we had not heard since the war began, our murdered friend Kang Sung-Kap, our loved ones in the North...

It had been over six years since I last saw my parents. The full realization came to me at that moment that I might never see them again. The tide of grief I had shored up all those years broke through the barriers I had erected. I gave in to the overwhelming urge to cry.

During this hour of weeping I experienced once more the wonder of God's grace. I had lost one family, but God had provided me with a new one. This stern seminary principal, whom I had found so difficult to approach, opened himself up to me now and willingly became my new father. He spoke to me with kindness, patting my shoulder. Tentatively at first, then more confidently, he put his arm around me and comforted me.

Had I looked up, I would have known that I was not the only one in that family circle with tears. Separation from one's family is a common Korean experience. It is a tragedy every Korean understands and feels profoundly. The pain of separation has become a national characteristic of Koreans, in both the North and the South. And as long as that pain remains, our hope persists for a re-unified Korea.

No longer free

The first six months of our marriage were—dare I say this?—absolutely terrible. I felt as though I were in prison. Suddenly I no longer felt free to do as I pleased, to wander where I wished, to visit friends, or even to disappear into the mountains for days without anyone asking me where I had been.

We had only one very small room to call home, a fact which no doubt increased my feeling of captivity. But after years of living alone , I realized what it was like to have responsibility for another human being. Suddenly, at the age of 29, another person depended on me. Now and forever.

I must have frightened Shin-Jah, raving about Kim Sakkat, whom I had once adopted as a model for my life, about my anti-establishment tendencies, about my theories holding every institution to be inherently corrupt.... She must have wondered what she had married.

During those first six months, I felt I had made a serious mistake. But once again, although I didn't know why I had taken such a step, God knew.

Shin-Jah soothed my frightened spirit and healed my wandering mind.

She reorganized my thinking and made it a pleasure to settle down. My wife created for me a home with a warmth and security I had never known before. In time, she bore me three daughters and we became a family.

As fearful of marriage as I was in the beginning, it has been an experience for which I will thank God for as long as I live.

A pattern of resistance

I resisted ordination even longer than I resisted marriage. Somehow, I couldn't see myself as an ordained minister. I felt I was not good enough, not stable enough, not wise enough for such a vocation. I also felt that once ordained, there is no turning back, no changing my mind.

When we finally returned to Seoul after the war, I was hired as assistant minister at Kyongdong Presbyterian Church while continuing graduate studies. The session of the church repeatedly asked about my ordination; every time I found an excuse for procrastinating.

One day my father-in-law simply announced to me that he had submitted my application for ordination to the Presbytery, adding that I should not miss the following week's meeting. I had forgotten how annoying it can be to have a father!

I have no resentment, though. My father-in-law, a very perceptive person, recognized part of my nature. In any matter of real importance, I always find myself torn between willingness and resistance. When I see things that need to be done, I am willing to help. But in the next moment, another part of me says, "Why me? Others are more competent...." My father-in-law also recognized that once I have made a commitment, I will do my best. In my ordination, he decided that he had better take the first step for me. My life would never have been as exciting and fulfilling had I not been ordained in the Kyung-Gi Presbytery in November 1954.

In the middle of controversy

Throughout my life I have constantly tried to escape from strife and turmoil. Yet no matter where I went, I have always ended up in the middle of controversy—even if the controversy was hardly ever of my own making.

In this case, I married into controversy.

At the time I married, my father-in-law was the most controversial figure in the Korean church. In fact, the church into which I was ordained, the newly-created Presbyterian Church in the Republic of Korea, was a direct consequence of that controversy.

Kim Chai-Choon had been converted to Christianity as a young man. After graduation from Bible school in Seoul, and from seminary in Tokyo, he had taken graduate studies at Princeton Seminary in the USA. In the early 1930s, a major theological rift there ended with Professor John G. Machen leaving Princeton and founding Westminster Seminary.

The Koreans studying in Princeton at the time also split into conservative and liberal factions. Kim Chai-Choon remained in Princeton; another Korean, Park Hyung-Yong followed Machen to Westminster. When these two students returned to Pyongyang (now the capital of North Korea), the conservative Park was given a teaching position by the missionaries who ran the seminary, while Kim had to seek employment elsewhere. (One of those places was the high school in Manchuria which I later attended.) Pyongyang Seminary was eventually closed down by the Japanese.

When Kim Chai-Choon returned to Seoul, Christians there wanted to organize a non-academic Bible college. The Japanese granted permission, on the basis of a yearly review. This modest institution, founded by my father-in-law, offered the only theological education available anywhere in Korea during World War II. After the war, with the North now communist, the Assembly of the Korean Presbyterian Church turned that Bible college into Chosun Theological Seminary.

In the meantime, Park Hyung-Yong had arrived in Seoul. He sought to re-open the Pyongyang Seminary as the Presbyterian Church's official theological training school. But to justify this, he needed to convince the church of the inadequacy of Chosun Seminary.

He found his opportunity when a student studying under Kim Chai-Choon showed Park his Old Testament class notes.

My future father-in-law, it appeared, was teaching what in European and North American seminaries had become a routine subject, historical and form criticism. This included the theory, for example, that four distinct literary "traditions" can be identified in the Pentateuch, the first five books of the Bible. But for Park Hyung-Yong and most missionaries of the time, this teaching amounted to blasphemy. It implied the existence of editors who manipulated and rearranged biblical passages. Park accused Kim Chai-Choon of heresy at the Presbyterian Assembly. A heated debate erupted about the authority of the scriptures as the inspired Word of God.

It did not help Chosun Seminary's case that they also taught such supposedly "liberal" theologians as Karl Barth and Emil Brunner.

Kim Chai-Choon never considered himself a radical. During that controversy, he produced a 30-page theological confession, setting out his beliefs in detail. He distributed this in the Korean church. He also sent a copy to the "mother church," the Presbyterian headquarters in the USA. After carefully studying this document, the American church concluded that this was indeed very standard Reformed theology.

Most of the American missionaries in Korea sided with Park Hyung-Yong, however. They criticized their home church for being too liberal. One of the sad aspects of mission history has been the way some missionaries have used the mission field to create their own conservative kingdoms. As a result, young churches are often deliberately prevented from achieving maturity and independence in the faith.

Canadian missionaries did not always see eye-to-eye with their American counterparts. In this controversy, they supported Kim Chai-Choon. The United Church of Canada, having studied Kim Chai-Choon's confession, concluded that it was a perfectly acceptable, even eloquent, portrayal of Christian faith and practice.

But the Assembly of the Jesus Presbyterian Church in Korea concluded that Kim Chai-Choon was a danger to the faith. They suspended him from his ministerial functions. Furthermore, they decreed, any ordained graduates of Chosun Seminary who did not reject Kim Chai-Choon's teachings, in writing, would be similarly suspended.

A small but significant group of pastors and lay people felt that there was no longer room for them in that Presbyterian Church. In 1953 they established the Presbyterian Church in the Republic of Korea, or PROK.

Kim Chai-Choon himself never coveted ecclesiastical power. He was elected moderator of the PROK only once, for one year, two decades later.

The founding of the PROK signalled the beginning of a new theological era in Korea. Until then, theology was rarely discussed or debated. It was simply something to accept from the teachings of missionaries, or to learn at European or North American schools. As a result of this doctrinal controversy, the question: "What is theology for *Koreans*?" became keenly pertinent. People discovered a rich variety of theological roots. Books were translated, articles and papers were written and published, top-level scholars were invited on lecture tours. The Korean church was coming of age.

The PROK is still the only Presbyterian church in Korea (there are now five Presbyterian denominations) which ordains women as elders and ministers. The PROK has been at the forefront of developing an indigenous theology, that is, a theology suited to the special experience and needs of Koreans. The first "minjung" (meaning "people") theologians in Korea came from the PROK.

When in The United Church of Canada I hear people raising the issue of the authority of the scriptures, it is like *déjà vu* for me. I have seen much insensitivity and ambition justified in the name of divine verbal inspiration. I suppose all Christians have to pass through this stage at one time in their lives. Quoting scripture verses to criticize those who disagree with us is a strong temptation. But I pray that we can be blessed with more maturity, so that the power of biblical witness can transform us into faithful, loving persons who have put childish ways behind us.

Ministry among the very poor

One Saturday morning, after I had served some two years as assistant minister in Kyongdong Church, we learned that a friend of ours had died. His outspoken defence of the poor in his community had split his original congregation. Rejected by those who believed their pastor ought to uphold the status quo, he gathered his faithful into a new, very poor congregation. Unfortunately he developed kidney problems.

The grieving congregation invited me to preach at his church the next day. Sung-Am Church was housed in a poorly constructed temporary building, with a destitute manse behind the pulpit. When I arrived there, my friend's body still lay in the manse.

After the service, the elders asked whether I would replace him as their minister. As a friend, I would understand that the congregation had a responsibility to take care of his family. His wife, three children, his mother and his brother were all living in the manse, with no other place to go.

I accepted the call. And so my family and I plunged ourselves into this desperately poor community. The war had taken a terrible toll. Of approximately 100 parishioners, half were widows. Industries did not yet provide sufficient work; the few industries that did exist exploited labor which was plentiful and therefore cheap.

Since the manse of our new church was already occupied, my wife and I had to find some other housing. The cheapest place we could find was the servants' quarters in an old traditional house. We moved into one cramped room behind the gate with our two little daughters. Our youngest daughter was born while we served this church.

Although our parishioners were embarrassed to have their pastor living in such inadequate quarters, they really had no choice. After the service every Sunday, the elders counted the collection, paid the outstanding bills, and then handed the remainder to my wife, trying to escape before we could see how little it was. Financially, this was the most difficult period of our married life.

But there were also benefits. We had a marvelous congregation. The people were so kind, so loving, so grateful for the service we could render. These were open-minded and active church members. We had a community of support and prayer. This church was too poor for pride or for pettiness— diseases which have consumed many other churches. We had no doctrinal disputes, no attempts by some to force their own opinions down the throats of others. These people would help each other as much as they could, and would pray for each other when nothing else could be done.

God blessed that church richly in ways that money cannot buy. And I was especially blessed, because it was there, not in the seminary, where I learned how to be a pastor.

Pushed out of the nest once more

Canada might never have had to contend with Lee Sang-Chul, if his father-in-law had not constantly sought ways to improve him.

In 1958, Kim Chai-Choon spent six months visiting churches and colleges in Canada. He received an honorary doctorate at Union College in Vancouver. On his return, he advised me that Union College would offer me a scholarship in 1960, to come and study in Canada. This was too exciting an offer to turn down.

In the meantime, however, I was appointed secretary for student work at the PROK headquarters. When 1960 came around, I faced the same dilemma my assassinated friend Kang Sung-Kap had faced years before. The students came to me and said, "This is the most important period in history for Korean students. You cannot go at this time."

I don't think any of us, in those days, believed that students could topple a government. This was still eight years before student rebellions frightened North American and European governments. And in our situation, the rule of law did not restrain the forces of order.

But on April 25, 1960, defying martial law, all university faculties, including professors, gathered in Seoul. Ordinary citizens and even soldiers joined the demonstrations. President Syngman Rhee found himself forced to resign the day after, and was soon exiled from the country.

After his resignation, the students immediately declared that they had no further interest in politics. Their main aim, they said, was that government should allow academic freedom and fair and honest elections. Their declaration set me free to come to Canada.

No one foresaw then that the democratically elected government of Chang Myon would be toppled in a CIA-inspired *coup d'étât* just one year later, on May 16, 1961.

But by then, I hadstarted to spend two years studying at The United Church of Canada's Union College on the gloriously beautiful campus of the University of British Columbia.

A stranger in Canada

Had I known that Canada would one day become my home and naturalized land, I am quite certain that I would have torn up my airline ticket and stayed with my wife and children in Seoul.

I suffered the long flight over the Pacific in silence, letting my mind review my life. I concluded that God had meant me to be a wanderer, a man without a home. I comforted myself with the thought that Jesus too had had no place to lay his head, that the children of Israel wandered for 40 years in the desert, without a country to call their own. And is the church not supposed to be on the move—ever vigilant, in the world but not of it?

If so, then I was setting a good example. I was flying to Canada, the country of most of the missionaries with whom I had been associated. I carried a cardboard suitcase full of used clothes. In my pocket I had ten US dollars, and a cheque for five Canadian dollars, given to me as a going-away present by one of the missionaries. I had no idea how far this money would take me.

But the excitement I had felt for weeks before my departure had turned into sadness and anxiety. Already I was feeling desperately lonely. I wondered how I would survive the next two years. But our financial situation meant I could neither return for holidays, nor bring my family with me.

Very late in the evening, we landed at Vancouver International Airport. I watched the other passengers eagerly preparing to disembark, while I sat numbly, wishing the plane could take me back to Korea. Outside its doors, a totally new and different life awaited me.

Then the stewardess asked me if I needed any help, and I realized that the moment had come.

I was the last one to leave the plane.

Exploring the situation

Though still jet-lagged, I was in a much more hopeful mood the next morning. I admired my room, bathed in the brilliance of the sun beaming through a window without curtains. It was cozy, equipped with desk, bookshelves, closet, cupboards and a sink, in addition to the steel-spring bed. Modest, but plenty of space for a single person and quite adequate for my academic needs. I wondered what student life would be like for a man almost 40 years old.

It was Sunday. I attended a service in the school's chapel, on the advice of Dr. Reg Wilson, the professor who had welcomed me at the airport. I realized that it would take me some time to become accustomed to operating completely in the English language.

I spent the afternoon walking around the enormous campus of the University of British Columbia. The beauty of the nature surrounding me

The partially-finished Union College, now part of the Vancouver School of Theology, where the author spent the winter of 1961.

was astonishing. I wished that I could show this place to my family. I imagined my girls running up and down the hillsides, picking the flowers that were still blooming everywhere, even at this time of year.

A long path led from the campus to the beach far below. During the year to come, one of my favorite pastimes would be to walk along this beach and look across the rolling waves towards Asia.

On Monday, I met Dr. William Taylor, the principal of Union College. His wife offered to take me into town to shop for items I would need to set myself up on campus. When I told her how much money I had, she looked rather shocked. The principal gave me some money to tide me over, and later arranged for a monthly allowance of forty dollars.

I had no cause to complain. My tuition, room and board were all taken care of by my scholarship. To supplement that monthly allowance, I found a job in the library, working two nights a week.

Walking on the campus, I saw an oriental man passing by. I asked if he was Korean. He was Japanese, and in too much of a hurry to talk. Over the next few weeks, I approached every oriental I met; all were Chinese or Japanese.

Someone suggested I inquire at the International Students' Centre on campus. I discovered one other Korean registered at UBC. I telephoned him to introduce myself, and was invited to his home some weeks later. There I met Dr. Shim, his wife and family, as well as another Korean medical doctor, Dr. Oh and his wife. Their two families and I were the only Koreans in the whole of Vancouver in 1961.

This made Korean acquaintances all the more precious. The two families and I became close friends. I was often invited to their homes, where we could speak our own language, discuss Korean politics and eat meals that were as authentically Korean as possible—considering that the only oriental grocery stores in Vancouver were all Chinese.

Student life turned out to be quite pleasant. As always, I loved reading. Listening to lectures in English proved more difficult, though my comprehension improved as months passed. Speaking English was still a chore. It was frustrating not to be able to express my thoughts clearly. I often felt that professors and students, though very patient, humored me, pretending that what I had said made sense, though their comments showed that they had usually misunderstood me.

Writing English was the most difficult of all.

Comparisons of two societies

Constantly I made mental comparisons between Canada and Korea. On a weekend retreat, I was amazed to see professors cooking meals, cleaning up and working around the cottage we stayed in, while students sat around and talked. Yet the professors seemed to be enjoying themselves, humming tunes, telling jokes and smiling.

They contrasted sharply with Korean professors, who were usually bloated with self-importance. They vaunted their superiority, looking down on those over whom they had authority. These Canadian professors had a comfortingly humble and unselfish style. I became convinced that this had something to do with the difference between an atmosphere of authoritarianism, as found in Korea, and a free and open society, like Canada.

The difference extended also to the students, though I reacted to them with varied emotions. The first time a Canadian student invited me for a cup of coffee, he left the cafeteria ahead of me, paying only for his own cup. In Korea, the person inviting would pay for both, or suffer a serious loss of respect. Did freedom have to include the sacrifice of courtesy?

One morning at breakfast, my co-residents were doubled over with mischievous laughter. They had raided the neighboring Anglican seminary at 2 o'clock the previous night. They warned me to keep my windows and doors locked that night, in case of a possible Anglican retaliation. The counter-attack came as predicted. Several of our students found themselves abandoned some 50 miles from UBC campus, wearing only their pajamas. It took them until noon the next day to hitch-hike back.

These students seemed so free of care. They partied to exhaustion. It amazed me that they still managed to get their studies done. At first I felt envious of the opportunities they enjoyed. But as time passed, I felt more and more convinced that they had it *too* good.

I thought of them as straight, tall, well-nurtured trees. In contrast, Korean young people are like trees bent out of shape by the violent elements, their roots anchored in cracks between rocks. Straight trees have their merits, but I wondered how they would stand up to the Korean environment. Twisted trees have their own rugged beauty.

Still, I learned to appreciate their sincerity. Vancouver can be as drab as it is beautiful. When October brought endless rain, and I could no longer walk along the ocean shore, my loneliness sometimes got the better of me. Always, some of the students would notice my mood and try to cheer me up.

One time during the year, the letters from my wife, which had until then faithfully arrived once a week, stopped for three weeks. Every day I rushed to the mailbox; every day I was disappointed.

I began to worry that something serious might have happened, and wrote a concerned letter to my father-in-law. Replies arrived from both my father-in-law and my wife on the same day. There was no particular tragedy, they indicated, but my wife was having serious difficulties making ends meet. She was working for a Christian publishing house, but her salary didn't cover the family expenses. She had moved several times to find cheaper accommodation. I was so depressed, I was tempted to quit my studies and return immediately.

The students noticed my melancholy. I told them about my wife's situation. Following the next weekly chapel service, the students came to me with all the offerings and told me to send them to my wife. I was unable to hold back my tears. The love and encouragement I received from these Canadian students gave me the strength to endure.

Adventure into central Canada

At Christmas time, when the other students left campus for their homes, my loneliness became unbearable. Dr. Taylor and his wife invited me to their home.

As we had lunch on December 22, the university chaplain rushed in, out of breath, explaining that he had been looking for me everywhere. In his hands he held two airline tickets to Toronto, where a gathering of the Canadian Student Christian Movement was taking place over Christmas.

I was to go in one hour!

At that gathering in Toronto, I met four Koreans I had known in the student movement at home. They were now studying at Emmanuel College in Toronto, and at McGill University in Montreal. Knowing that other friends shared my experience was very reassuring.

To crown this memorable Christmas, we went to Niagara Falls. Living so close to it now, Niagara Falls has lost some of its magic. But arriving there at the end of 1961 after two hours of driving in the snow, I was mesmerized by the sight.

I walked to the edge of the falls, as close as I could safely get to the water. Forgetting how ridiculous I felt in my borrowed, oversized winter coat, I stared at the millions of gallons of water rushing into the depths.

I was hypnotized. The power and endlessness there overwhelmed me with awe. How mighty are the works of God, I thought, and how stupidly we humans destroy them.

Invitations to speak

Canadian churches make good use of foreign students, I discovered, especially those from countries where Canadian churches send missionaries. At first I enjoyed all the attention I received. Almost every weekend I would be invited to local churches or to small groups to talk about Korea.

I was pleased at the interest shown for my country by Canadian Christians. At times I met people who knew Korea, or even Manchuria, and we could exchange reminiscences. At the very first student retreat I attended, I met a Canadian student, the son of a missionary, who had grown up in Manchuria. On another occasion, I met a doctor who had worked at the mission hospital in the Manchurian town where I had attended high school. At his home I was shown photographs of my old town, the church where I served as Sunday school superintendent, and my high school. More amazing yet, I found myself in a photograph of the student body!

One day, I answered a knock on my residence door. Before me stood the first Canadian I had ever met, George Bruce, once my high school principal. We reminiscenced about the times I had earned pocket money doing odd jobs around his house.

The joy of this reunion impressed on me the wonder of human relationships. These missionaries talked of Korea and Manchuria with an authentic love. For faith and love, I thought, there are no national boundaries.

But at other times, the attention became trying. For one thing, my English still left much to be desired. All week I struggled with complex concepts of theology, and then I was expected to give speeches on the weekends as well. It became terribly exhausting. If I spoke on a Sunday, well-meaning persons always invited me for a home-cooked meal. Pleasurable as the meals were, I was forced to struggle with my English, usually in the presence of additional guests!

I also discovered that most of the events were fund raising functions for Canadian missionaries. I was expected to encourage parishioners to increase their gifts of money.

These requests left me in a very awkward position. I appreciated all the positive things that missionaries have done for my country, and for me personally. But I had no intention of singing their praises without qualification. I felt then as I do now, that the Christian church needs to develop a new missiology which recognizes the value of indigenous cultures and traditions. As Western churches continue to send missionaries abroad, they must also learn to receive them.

Yet these things were difficult for me to explain in English, and it seemed inappropriate for me to question the role of missionaries at these fund raising events.

So after a while, I began to make excuses when I was invited to make speeches. I began to value my solitude, taking my favorite beach strolls, listening to the squawking of the seagulls, who asked for no replies and didn't mind if I spoke to them in Korean.

"Can Canadians really understand a life of poverty and oppression?" I wondered. "Canada is such a rich country. People here are not even aware of how fortunate they are."

I would sit on one of the many huge sun-bleached driftwood logs littering the seashore. If this were Korea, I thought, not a single piece of wood would remain on the entire beach. It would have been painstakingly collected and used for firewood.

Menial tasks

My scholarship did not cover the summer months. Theology students usually took charge of small country parishes which lacked any regular pastor. I thought I might enjoy this. However, after reflection, the college felt that it might be too difficult for me to handle the English language.

Reluctantly I agreed to take work as assistant caretaker of the school. It was a disappointment, however, since I regarded myself as a minister, not a janitor. I foresaw little pleasure in washing floors, cleaning toilets, and mowing lawns. It reminded me of the time after primary school, and again following my arrival in Seoul, when I had to do any type of odd job in order to survive.

In time, however, I found some serenity in that work. There is a kind of cleansing of the spirit which comes with menial labor. It is a humbling experience for anyone who feels himself to be worth more than others. I felt some repentance when I realized how unwilling I was to take on the servant role which followers of Christ should accept for themselves. I remembered how famous ministers and theologians had worked as dishwashers and gardeners to earn their education. Besides, there were two fringe benefits to this work: I had unlimited access to the library, and the wages were good enough that I could send money to my wife on a regular basis.

As the summer closed, I began to look forward to my final year of studies. Then I received a letter from Seoul, informing me that I had been chosen to receive another scholarship, this time for study at the graduate school at the Ecumenical Institute at Bossey, near Geneva, Switzerland. This school, organized by the World Council of Churches, would provide the opportunity of studying with students from every part of the globe, and of meeting world-renowned theologians first-hand. But it would prevent me from completing my degree in Vancouver. Or, at least, it would delay its completion for another year. I would have to endure an additional year's absence from my family.

My wife, happy for my sake for this once-in-a-lifetime opportunity, encouraged me to take the new scholarship. Her love made the decision all the harder, since I wanted so much to be with my family again. My supervising professor, Dr. George Tuttle, also encouraged me to go to Geneva. He promised to appeal to the board for permission to complete my thesis on my return, with full scholarship privileges.

That night I thanked God for the love, the kindness, the understanding which I had received, and for the opportunities coming my way. In the back of my mind, though, I think I harbored a suspicion that this might be preparation for some difficult and unpleasant task I would have to face later! I asked God what was in store for me. There was no answer. I think God was teaching me that the basis of faith is trust.

Sojourner in Switzerland

At Bossey, my ecumenical commitment was confirmed and deepened. I found a student body of some 50 ministers and professors from every part of the globe, of Eastern Orthodox, Roman Catholic and every variety of Protestant background. Although lectures and classes were interpreted into English, French and German, most students managed at least some English. I marvelled at the variety of accents with which students and professors spoke—I was relieved to find that my own English was far from the worst!

During the course of studies, we met many theologians whose works I had read years before. I had a private conversation with Emil Brunner; our class went to Basel to visit the retired Karl Barth; we were welcomed by Willem Visser t'Hooft, the co-founder and first General Secretary of the World Council of Churches.

The great Czech theologian Josef Hromadka lectured, warning us that the church is under greater danger from capitalism than from communism. When we visited John Calvin's cathedral in Geneva and saw the tiny congregation, almost lost within that enormous sanctuary, I began to think that perhaps he was right.

It was exciting to have so many viewpoints to consider. The Christian faith took on a vitality I had seldom felt before. I did not have to agree with these great theologians. I could challenge them, argue with them, and grow in the process. What impressed me was the humility of these people, their approachability, their inner security. It allowed them to hear my opinions without feeling threatened. I learned from this experience that those who are most insecure in their faith are usually also the most fanatical in pressing others to think like themselves.

During the Cuban Missile Crisis, we listened to the news every moment. The World Council of Churches issued a statement appealing to the Soviet Union to withdraw its missiles from Cuba. We students wished to support that statement, but an Orthodox priest from Rumania became extremely agitated. He accused us of being puppets of capitalist regimes.

I began to see a difference between students who grew up in freedom, and those who grew up enslaved by traditional, social, and political pressures. The actions of this Rumanian seemed strikingly similar to many students in my own country, who were afraid to criticize the Korean regime. Did it really make much difference whether a totalitarian government was communist or capitalist, I wondered? Both restricted the freedom of people.

Still, in those difficult situations the Christian church seems to thrive, against all expectations. Yet in the "free" world, like Western Europe or North America, church memberships are dwindling.

A further delay

It felt like coming home when I arrived in Vancouver in early March 1963. I dived wholeheartedly into my studies, realizing that the sooner I finished, the sooner I could return to Korea.

The Rev. Tad Mitsui, pastor of the Japanese United Church in Vancouver, was also working on his thesis at Union College. He was having a difficult time concentrating on it, because of his parish duties. From time to time he had asked me to preach for him at the church, which I was happy to do, though my Japanese was rather rusty after all these years.

In the summer of 1963, Tad Mitsui came to me with a proposition. He needed eight months undisturbed to finish his thesis. He asked me to stay longer in Vancouver, to relieve him temporarily of his parish duties.

It took me some time to reach a decision. I wanted to support my friend. I also wanted to get back to my family in Seoul.

But there was an additional hesitation. Although this was almost 20 years after Korean "liberation," and although I considered myself to be a rational adult, deep within me I could still feel traces of anti-Japanese sentiments. Could I overcome the anger and resentment left from my youth? In the end I agreed to stay, if only to exorcize some of the devils of prejudice still clouding my soul. Tad and Chico Mitsui's own open-mindedness helped me accept their proposal.

Once I began my eight-month ministry, I quickly realized that these were not the Japanese oppressors of my youth. These were, by and large, impoverished immigrants, seeking a better life in Canada. I learned much about Japanese immigration to Canada since the 19th century, the hardships of labor on farms and in the fishing industry, without regular salaries or the right to join unions. Some of them had even come to Canada because they disagreed with the militarization of their own country.

Yet here, I learned, many of them had suffered as much as I had during the war. The Canadian government had confiscated their properties and interned them for no crime other than being of Japanese descent.

I stopped seeing myself as a Korean and them as Japanese, and began instead to see myself as pastor and them as my congregation. Together, we learned that Christ's love transcends human boundaries. What I had learned intellectually at Bossey, I now learned emotionally as pastor of a Japanese congregation.

Like leaving home

By early May 1964, I had become rather attached to Vancouver. I had grown accustomed to the beauty of nature, the mountains, the flowers, the seashore, even the temperamental Vancouver weather, and I hoped to be able to show this city to my wife and daughters one day. But most of all, I had fallen in love with the people. I knew I would miss my professors, my fellow-students, my many Korean, Japanese, Chinese and Canadian friends. That made my departure for Korea difficult.

Of course, I looked forward to reunion with my family. At Kimpo International Airport in Seoul I was greeted by family and many friends. My wife looked radiant and full of joy. I could barely recognize my daughters. They had grown so much since I had left three years before. But without hesitation, they ran to their prodigal father and threw their arms around him.

And coming home again

My re-entry into the Korean church mainstream was more difficult, although my old friends helped in every respect. My old friend Kang Won-Yong and I started a Christian Academy, on the model of the German academies begun after the war. We felt a need for a place in Korea where people from all walks of life and from different political perspectives could meet, exchange opinions, make plans, and build a new faith in the future.

But my overseas experience had changed me. My views and opinions were no longer in tune with my former colleague. Conflicts surfaced.

A way out presented itself, an opportunity which would bring me back to Canada, but this time with my family. The town of Steveston, in the Richmond area of Vancouver, had been a pioneer village for Japanese immigration. In an earlier period, it had so many Japanese that they never needed to learn to speak English. But as the first generation immigrants grew older and the second and third generations became more Anglicized, the Japanese-speaking church there merged with the English-speaking United Church. Its pastor insisted that the church should seek a bilingual pastor to succeed him, for the sake of the older Japanese who had difficulties under-standing English. So I received a call to serve Steveston United Church.

My wife was apprehensive about moving to a foreign country, my children enthusiastic. Our friends were divided. Some encouraged me to go, recognizing my struggles at the Academy; others criticized me for seeking to escape while the future of Korea hung in the balance.

My father-in-law cast the deciding vote. He told me that so many missionaries had come from Canada to Korea, "God is giving you the chance to be a Korean missionary to Canada."

On a hot and humid July day in 1965, I took a sad-eyed wife and three ecstatic, fidgety daughters to the airport, bound for Canada.

A new homeland

Many Korean, Japanese and Canadian friends came to meet us at the airport. Dr. and Mrs. William Taylor welcomed us with such warmth, my family immediately felt at home. This relationship deepened over the years. It was Mrs. Taylor who chose our daughters' English names: Irene, Grace and Joy. Even today, the family thinks of them as our Canadian parents.

A few days later, the Steveston United Church congregation held a welcoming party. They showered us with cutlery, dishes, bed sheets and household necessities. My wife and I felt like newlyweds starting out in life.

The congregation included a number of fishermen. We prayed with those families when the men went out to sea. When they came back, they brought the choicest samples of their catch as gifts to their pastor. We always had a freezer full of seafood.

Our time at Steveston turned out to be bountiful. We felt at one with nature and with the people surrounding us. It did not take long for my wife to feel at home here, despite language difficulties. We lived in the most spacious house of our lives. The lawn was huge. In spring it filled up with daffodils; at Easter we decorated the cross in our church with them.

My wife decided to plant a garden, and started digging a corner of the lawn with a small hand shovel. Our Ukrainian neighbor, observing her slow progress, came over and helped her with his power tools. The earth was so rich, she didn't even need fertilizer. She grew generous harvests of cabbage, turnips, beans and many other vegetables. Soon we were eating home-grown kimchi!

Our daughters began school in "English as a Second Language" classes, taught by an experienced elderly lady. After six months, I complained that their English was not good enough and said in jest that I would send them back to Korea. They were not amused. Later, when I visited their school, I found several of their compositions posted in the hallway as good examples. I was impressed by my daughters' progress, and had to apologize for being too hasty in my criticism.

I was supremely happy in my parish. On Sunday mornings, I conducted an English-language service, and in the evening I preached in Japanese. The

Japanese services were held in the homes of parishioners. The number of those who could not follow English grew steadily smaller. Now it was mainly the older people, and they preferred to gather in more informal surroundings, where they could end the evening with good Japanese cooking.

The Lee family at the manse at Steveston United Church

Growing roots

Until 1965, Canada had no Korean immigration to speak of. But after Prime Minister Lester Pearson introduced new immigration policies, Korean immigrants began to arrive in Vancouver almost weekly.

Immigration authorities at the airport were totally unprepared for this influx. Some Koreans told me they were even asked what language Koreans spoke! Since I was the only Korean pastor in town, immigration officers began to call me to the airport to interpret and to help people find lodgings or onward travel.

Life became increasingly complicated. Many of these people came as I had done the first time, with very little money. Often, we ended up feeding and lodging entire families in our home. Some, headed for Toronto or other parts of Canada, were stranded in Vancouver because they had missed their flight connections. One woman with three children called me because she had a fever. Though I arranged for my Korean doctor friend to look after her, I discovered that her hungry children refused to eat any Western food. As there were no Korean restaurants in Vancouver at that time, they came to eat at our house.

Some people arrived with wrong documents, or with mistakes on their forms; they were refused entry. I had to make long distance calls to relatives to bail them out. In a few cases, companies in Korea made fraudulent arrangements; some even gave my name and telephone number as a reference! One young lady had been falsely assured that she could obtain an American visa *after* she arrived in Canada—I had to page her sponsor, waiting for her at the Chicago airport, to get him to consult lawyers for her permit.

Our family life became more and more disrupted by telephone calls in the middle of the night. Sometimes it seemed as if we had tumbled into a soap opera.

In the meantime, the Korean community in Vancouver expanded enormously. I also became busy with the numerous problems that confront people trying to settle in. There were jobs to find, and unhappiness with the jobs available. There were strains in family life. Many suffered culture shock.

Someone coined a Korean term that might be translated "immigration disease," an apt designation for what I had to deal with. Some new arrivals discouraged their children from identifying themselves as Koreans, fearing that they would be considered "backward." Others organized parties every weekend to win friends or to break their loneliness. Some people took to drinking, and used their fists to back up irrelevant arguments.

Many frustrations were not dealt with, because Koreans felt it would hurt their pride to cry out. When I visited couples having marriage problems, they acted as though everything were going beautifully. Then the next day, the women called me on the phone, sobbing so hard they couldn't say anything. Once I had to find refuge for a wife who had been badly beaten by her husband.

Stresses in the Korean community were not being resolved. I began to wonder about my role as pastor. What was the purpose of an immigrant church? I prayed with and for the people. I read and re-read the Gospels for clues.

For me, the life of Jesus had always been a life of healing. I wanted the church also to be a place of healing. I wanted the church to be the place where everyone, without inhibitions, could pour out their frustrations and stresses and pains of their lives. I wanted the church to be a place where people could renew their minds and redirect and revitalize their hopes.

I began to see why God might have originally sent me to Canada. God had thrust me into the Japanese immigrant community, almost against my will, so that I would personally learn about the problems that all immigrants face.

I began to see my task less as a missionary to English Canadians than as a counsellor, helping those who wished to integrate into Canadian society, helping Koreans make a positive contribution which would enrich their adopted country.

Beginning a Korean church

Our home became a place for many Koreans to drop in, to gather for conversations or meals. Koreans from all walks of life attended, both Christians and non-Christians. Before eating meals, of course, I said grace. But otherwise, I tried not to make non-Christians feel uncomfortable.

One day, during such a gathering at our house, someone suggested that we should have Korean church services together. We rented the student common room at Union Theological College, and began to meet one Sunday a month. The first time we met, about 50 people showed up. Only about ten had any Christian background.

Since we had few Korean Bibles or hymn books, I used Korean folk songs known to everyone during the service. Usually I gave a short, five-minute talk—not a sermon in the formal sense of the word. The rest of the time was for fellowship, the main reason so many came.

When more Christians arrived, at subsequent meetings, they criticized me for using folk songs in worship services. But singing folk songs was theologically appropriate, I felt. Praising God should combine the personal, cultural, traditional and religious elements of our lives. Until recently, there were no real Korean hymns. The missionaries thought that European culture had a monopoly on sacred music. All the hymns Koreans had used were actually translations of Western hymns. That meant we were singing with our minds, but not with our hearts. To my mind, Korean folk songs served better to bond our small community together.

Some months later, a committee was formed, of Christians only, to organize the services. One of their decisions was to hold the religious part of our gathering in the chapel. I was not happy about this decision. I felt it would alienate some who would no longer feel comfortable attending the worship part of our gatherings. Although our services had been somewhat unorthodox, they were a sign of the Gospel reaching into people's lives.

As an increasing number of Christian Koreans came to Vancouver, the Korean church in Vancouver became shaped into more traditional molds, and the Korean community became more segregated. I tried as hard as I could to resist this development.

At another monthly gathering, some other immigrants suggested that we create a Korean society, like the ones in some US cities. Despite my objections, a Korean-Canadian Cultural Association was founded. I felt another potential wedge had been driven between two diverging groups.

I insisted that a member of the Korean Association always be invited to meetings of the church council, because I felt strongly that the church should keep an open ear to the problems and joys as well as criticisms of the wider community which it serves. I am proud that Canada's first Korean church, Vancouver Korean United Church, was born as an integral part of the Korean social community.

All this increased my workload astronomically. Officially, I was still the pastor of a mainly English-speaking congregation, with responsibility for Japanese parishioners. Korean work, which took more and more of my time, should have been strictly extra-curricular. I am still grateful to my congregation at Steveston United for being so understanding of my dilemma. They never criticized, but rather gave me encouragement.

By 1966, I had unintentionally become a *trilingual* pastor. On Sunday mornings I preached in English, in the afternoons in Korean, and in the evenings in Japanese. Nor could I simply repeat the same sermon for each group. Each of the three was a distinct community, not only in language, but in its problems, understandings and level of spiritual maturity. My wife frequently teased me that I mixed up all three languages in my sermons. I never noticed. Nor did anyone ever complain. But when Prime Minister Trudeau first introduced multiculturalism as an official government policy, I thought I could teach him a lot about the subject.

A multicultural church and nation

The image of Canada as a "mosaic" rather than "melting pot" appeals to those who wish to belong to this marvelous country, but who cannot and should not forsake the culture and the people from which they originate. I wish to be Canadian, without having to deny that I am a Korean.

This is why I believe that The United Church of Canada is such a genuinely Canadian church. It was brought into being by the conviction that only a strong broad fellowship could meet the needs of Canada's scattered and diverse population. The United Church had always embraced groups and individuals of different backgrounds. Maybe what we need now is a "theology of multiculturalism."

The media have emphasized our church's divisions in recent months. But I see the situation from a different perspective. The United Church has attracted a wonderful diversity of people, who have helped to enrich our community and our country. We must not fear this diversity. It is God-given, a blessing to be embraced with thanksgiving. Through the challenge of this diversity, we will grow stronger and more united. And in the process, we will help Canada to be what it already is: a microcosm of the world itself, the wonderful, miraculous kaleidoscope of God's creation.

Citizenship classes

I first began to reflect on these matters while working with senior Japanese immigrants. They had been in Canada for 10, 15, even 20 years, without ever receiving Canadian citizenship. Their problem was language. They could handle neither English nor French very well. Yet they felt Canadian in every other respect, had contributed to the Canadian economy through their work, and wished to die and be buried in Canada.

I spoke to a citizenship court judge about their plight. He gave me a pile of textbooks and suggested I teach them enough to pass the test. Soon I had about 30 students in my "citizenship class," ranging in age from 60 to 80. We met once a week for several months.

The lessons proceeded not unlike a kindergarten. I would ask them the names of the provinces, capital cities, the current prime minister, year of confederation, and so on. They had to answer me in correct English. We drilled the answers as a group and individually. Then the next week, we had to go over the same material again, because these aging minds had a very short memory span.

On the appointed day, the whole class went to see the judge. Some of my charges were so scared they could hardly speak above a whisper.

The judge called them into his office one by one for their interviews. At the end, he called me in privately and told me that he had a difficulty. About half of the group passed the interview. But the other half, with the best of will, he just couldn't approve with a clear conscience. I told him that it would be a terrible loss of face for them if he failed half of the class! He asked how I would solve this dilemma. I promised that if he awarded them their citizenship, I would make it my responsibility to give them further language training. The judge was delighted with this solution.

My Japanese friends were overjoyed. They came to the citizenship ceremony wearing their finest, and when they were pronounced Canadian, many cried openly—which for a Japanese is almost taboo. In his speech to them, the judge admitted that half of them would not have passed but for Pastor Lee, and admonished them to continue their lessons with me.

We had a celebration at the church for these new "senior citizens." They came with children, grandchildren and tons of the most delicious food. I was treated like a hero, and received a new suit as a gift of gratitude.

This experience, more than anything else, showed me the value that immigrants place on becoming citizens of Canada. I thought of the hundreds of thousands of Koreans who to this very day have been unable to obtain citizenship in Japan, even after living there for several generations. I also thought of many Canadians who never think twice about their good fortune in being citizens of this country. I came to appreciate the openness and inclusiveness of Canada.

Yet I myself was not yet a Canadian citizen.

The judge was puzzled to see a non-Canadian expending so much effort helping others to become Canadian, without wanting the same privilege for himself. He gave me application forms to take home for my whole family.

We passed our interviews in the spring, and became Canadian citizens in the fall of 1969.

The national pressures

New arrivals from Korea could not find employment in Vancouver. News began to reach our Korean community that there were better job opportunities in Toronto, Canada's industrial heartland. One by one, families began to move east. Many of our friends disappeared.

From The United Church's national offices in Toronto, I was constantly being asked for advice about Korean church affairs. It seemed that there was a lot of in-fighting going on in Toronto. This was distressing news. I had been sick of the inter-denominational quarrels in Korea, yet here the same disease was repeating itself. A Korean congregation had been founded in Toronto in 1967, a year after ours in Vancouver. In less than two years, a Presbyterian church split from it. Then an additional split started an independent church.

When a vacancy developed at the Korean United Church in Toronto, I received a call to become their pastor. Neither my wife nor I wanted to leave Vancouver, where we now felt at home. I asked my father-in-law for advice. He wrote back wondering why I would wish to jeopardize my health and sanity by getting involved in a Korean community racked with feuding.

That was almost a dare. I had long dreamed of a broadminded church, drawing together the various church traditions which brought Christianity to Korea, and uniting them in a socially conscious community. With some difficulty, I decided to go.

I feared that my Korean congregation would take my decision badly, and they did. Some got angry and shouted at me. All tried to persuade me to change my mind. As they had been able to pay very little towards my salary, they didn't know if they would be able to support a new minister.

The Japanese congregation was sad too, but respected my decision. They understood that I would wish to serve my own people full-time.

What surprised me the most was the reaction of the English-speaking congregation. I thought they might be the least concerned about my going. At the final service, however, there were tears in many eyes. One of the Sunday school teachers and choir members became so emotional that she had to leave the sanctuary even before the service ended. My wife was crying too. Though these people were so different from her in almost every way, both she and I had become attached to the kind and warm congregation of Steveston United Church.

I left Vancouver more convinced than ever of the power of the Holy Spirit to cleanse our enmities and remove our divisions, and the powerful love of our Lord Jesus Christ, who can overcome our racial, cultural, social and sexual barriers.

Thrust into controversy

When we left Vancouver by car in July 1969, camping across the wide expanse of Canada, I felt confident, even though I knew that the Korean congregation I was going to had experienced a lot of conflict. I still felt warm from the farewells given us by our three congregations and our many friends in Vancouver. What a change since that first lonely day in Canada!

All the way across Canada, we stopped in any cities where Koreans lived. I encouraged them to keep the Korean community together, no matter how small. In larger centers like Edmonton and Winnipeg, I talked to Koreans about establishing a church. Everywhere I went, I delivered the same sermon: "Don't duplicate the denominational fights of Korea. Don't divide the Korean people living here by setting up separate churches."

In Toronto, I plunged into my work without hesitation. I was the first, and therefore most experienced, Korean immigrant pastor in all of Canada. Our congregation grew rapidly as more Koreans arrived almost every week. At its peak, our church had a membership of about 500 families, complete with hard-working and experienced leaders, Christians who had been leaders before coming to Canada.

My Vancouver experience proved to be valuable training for my work in Toronto. From the beginning, my ministry was not limited just to the church building. I continued to work with immigrants. I helped many Koreans with paperwork and regulations. I interpreted for many in immigration interviews.

A lot of my time was taken up with counselling, trying to combat the "immigration disease" which afflicted so many. I intervened in family quarrels. I dealt with cases of wife-beating, depression and other symptoms of culture shock. I began to help with legal problems. Soon I spent a considerable amount of time interpreting in court, mostly for minor problems such as traffic violations, rent disputes, and divorce cases. Inside and outside the church, I began to be recruited to serve on committees and boards. Work with the local Presbytery and The United Church's national offices consumed more and more time. I began writing regular columns for Korean language newspapers, and started producing *Voice of Hope*, a Korean-language radio broadcast.

All these activities were a joy to me. I felt secure in the knowledge that I had finally arrived at the place God wanted me to be. I was good at what I was doing, and I enjoyed what I did.

The Korean crisis

Then events half way around the world began to catch up with me. Letters from Korea told me things the Canadian news media never mentioned. These letters increased in urgency, and then turned into telephone calls. "Help us," they kept saying to me. "Do something for us."

The calls and letters came from friends I had left behind in Korea. Korea's nightmare had returned. My friends were being arrested and tortured. I myself was safe in Canada, a Canadian citizen and a proud community leader. But those I left behind in Korea were suffering again, and that knowledge made me feel guilty.

I realized once more how interconnected are our lives, how meaningless are geographical distances in this global village. I realized again that when Jesus speaks of "neighbors," he means anyone who needs us, anywhere in the world. My problem was that God had presented me with an assignment for which I had no competence. I had no idea how to respond.

Martial law in Korea

History was repeating itself in Korea, with a vengeance. President Park Chung-Hee, who had taken office through a CIA-inspired coup, followed Syngman Rhee's example. To allow himself to run for a third term of office, like Syngman Rhee, he tried to change the constitution. People became angry. Students demonstrated. Opposition parties were in an uproar.

A number of church leaders became involved. Kim Chai-Choon, my father-in-law, chaired a committee opposed to these constitutional changes.

All efforts failed, however. On April 19, 1971, Park was re-elected for a third term after a dirty election campaign, narrowly defeating his rival, Kim Dae-Jung.

Park began to use the military to raid campuses. He arrested students by the thousands. He also sacked teachers and professors, and instituted what he called "re-education camps." My father-in-law was forced into early retirement as principal of Hankuk Seminary.

Every campus in the country seethed with revolt. I traveled to Korea in September of that year, having been invited as visiting lecturer for a one month course in pastoral counselling. I attended the General Assembly of the PROK and could feel the tension in the air.

Suddenly, on October 17, 1971, shortly after my return to Canada, Park declared martial law. He introduced the so-called "Yushin" (Restoration) Constitution, which allowed him to dissolve parliament and place opposition members into prison under brutal torture. He sent the military with tanks and heavy weapons into the campuses to restore order. He closed all universities. He increased the power and scope of his secret police, the Korean Central Intelligence Agency (KCIA), who kept close tabs on any real or imagined opposition, whether from politicians, students, professors or religious leaders.

I was shocked. After long association with the universities, in the student movement and as student pastor, I suffered with every item of news that reached me. I felt helpless, yet I had to do something. For lack of a better idea, I decided to publish an open letter to President Park Chung-Hee, denouncing his actions and demanding that he withdraw from the universities and re-establish academic freedom. I called the editor of a Korean newspaper in Toronto, who said by all means to bring him the letter. But when I arrived at his office, he said he had contacted his paper's headquarters in Seoul; they told him not to print my letter. The man was obviously embarrassed, but his face betrayed fear. There was no sense in arguing. A corrupt Korean government could intimidate Koreans, even in Canada.

Another Korean weekly had been founded only six months before. I talked to its publisher. We agreed to convene a forum to discuss the Korean situation. I expected some 12 to 14 Korean ministers, cultural association leaders and others to attend, but only two people showed up. Undeterred, we decided to condemn the military dictatorship and demand the restoration of academic freedom.

Canadian repercussions

The next thing I heard was that the Korean embassy had personally attacked this publisher, threatening his family members back in Korea. I began to realize the lengths to which Park Chung-Hee's government would go. I heard that a couple of elders in my church had been put under pressure because of me.

One day, the Korean ambassador came to Toronto and slandered me personally, in a public speech to the Korean community. Friends told me that he suggested that I should resign my ministry. According to the ambassador, if I had such a keen interest in politics, I should become a politician back in Korea.

Needless to say, I was fuming!

The following Sunday, an embassy official attended our church. After the service, he came into the fellowship hall to share in our coffee time. When I saw him, I lost control of my temper. Blindly, I shouted at him, right in front of my parishioners. He was highly embarrassed and left the church quickly. The entire hall stared at me in silent disbelief.

That evening, I prayed for God's forgiveness. How could I have been so stupid in front of my people? What kind of example was I setting? I knew that my concern for what was going on in Korea was right. I knew that I was right to be angry at the Korean embassy's actions here in Canada. But my conduct had not been appropriate for a minister of the church. Was it motivated by guilt for my good life here in Canada, while my brothers and sisters suffered in Korea?

International coordination

The few of us outside of Korea actively engaged in the cause of justice and human rights soon realized that we had to coordinate actions among ourselves, so as not to become isolated and victimized by Korean government agents.

A number of former colleagues and friends were also living outside Korea at that time. Oh Jae-Shik was working with the Christian Conference of Asia, located in Tokyo. He was in a good position to get information quickly from Korea. Park Sang-Jung worked at the World Council of Churches in Geneva; he could quickly disseminate news around the world, in English as well as Korean. We had friends in key positions in New York, Los Angeles, and several countries in Europe. All of them could channel information to mainline churches, in countries that might use their influence with the Korean government to improve human rights.

The first chance to test our network came in 1973. A group of prominent pastors in Korea had prepared a statement, handed out to the thousands of worshippers at the early morning Easter service at Nam-San (South Mountain) in Seoul. Following that, in May, a group of Christian leaders published "The Korean Christian Manifesto." Before the KCIA could arrest the pastors involved, that statement had already been circulated to Japan, Europe and North America. It appeared in a number of church and secular newspapers in different parts of the world.

With the press in Korea totally censored, the government was surprised how this news could have gotten around so quickly! Telegrams of support for Korean churches began arriving at the Blue House from around the world. A number of Korean embassies received inquiries from the governments of their host countries about the information they had received from churches.

I realized then that quick, coordinated and effective action could be far more helpful to my friends than shouting in anger at anyone.

In our *Voice of Hope* radio program, broadcast for half an hour every Saturday in Toronto, we always read whatever news we received from Korea. The Korean embassy in Ottawa carefully monitored these broadcasts, and often accused us of spreading lies. I learned later that at times they genuinely believed we had fabricated the information, because they had not received it themselves. Sometimes they confirmed the facts as much as a week later, after making specific inquiries in Seoul. They became extremely suspicious of our efficiency, and began a more concentrated investigation of my connections in Korea.

Our friends inside Korea began to warn us to exercise extreme caution, and to check carefully every action we contemplated. If we made a wrong move, they said, those inside the country would suffer most.

As news of arrests, torture and harassment poured out of Korea, my anger reached new heights. I felt I could not keep quiet. If I did not preach justice, freedom and peace in my Sunday sermons, I would feel like a hypocrite. As in my youth, the knowledge of the evil afflicting my beloved Korea festered within me like a poison.

Some of my church members found it odd that I was so much engaged in this issue. They were used to a strict separation of politics and religion; they had trouble understanding a pastor who preached more about human rights in the here and now than about glory in the hereafter. My critics became more vocal, and tried to stop my activities.

I realized that I myself needed more spiritual preparation for this kind of work. I needed to be secure within myself, and to be able to explain my convictions to the believers in my congregation. I went back to the Bible once again, searching the scriptures, reading books of theology and social ethics. I began to learn more about the Christian's responsibility for a world in pain. I learned that Korea was not the only suffering country, that all people of the world are interconnected, and that if we do not care for each other we will ultimately destroy this planet, God's wonderful creation.

A split in the community

I was not able to persuade everyone in my congregation. Some people gradually absented themselves. Others began to avoid me. The session of the church raised questions. I began to feel cut off, lonely. My prayers became more intense. I asked God not to leave me alone, because this task was too great for one man. I asked God to send me other workers, to give more courage to those who already shared my concerns.

And my prayers were answered.

The number of people in my congregation who were willing to risk unpleasantness for the sake of justice began to grow. As our numbers grew, we created a Council for Democracy in Korea. From time to time this Council organized demonstrations in front of the Korean embassy in Ottawa, or its consulate in Toronto. The demonstrations were quite modest in size. The largest assembled only about 250 participants. But they made a point in public. They drew the attention of the media in Canada to the atrocities in Korea.

By 1974, too, the Korean government had made my father-in-law's situation so difficult that he decided to come to Toronto and live with us. Kim Chai-Choon was normally a gentle person, a quiet and shy man. But I can still see him when he first arrived; he said firmly, like a principal speaking of some misbehaving student, "We've got to remove that man!"

Three leaders of opposition to the Korean dictatorship of the 1970s: from left, Dr. Moon Jae-Rin, Dr. Kim Chai-Choon, and Sang-Chul Lee.

Sometime later, another senior church leader, the Rev. Dr. Moon Jae-Rin, father of two of my friends, also moved to Toronto. Our numbers strengthened. The Korean embassy began to think of Toronto as the centre of democratic opposition.

Yet our congregation was an anomaly among Korean-Canadians. Most Korean churches in Canada were unanimously conservative. Some Koreans told me that to participate in my activities could create problems for relatives in Korea. I tried hard to involve other pastors, but they were unwilling to cooperate. One day, a group of these pastors invited me for lunch. They criticized me, saying that my conduct could harm the church as a whole. What I was doing was political activity, they told me, and inappropriate for a man of the cloth. They strongly advised me to stop.

I realized then that I was alone. I listened patiently, but told them that it was my duty as a Christian to oppose injustice and dictatorship. I told them that God would not allow me to stop. And if they took their own leadership seriously, they ought to join me in my activities.

As it turned out, not all of them were hard-liners. My ministry was having an effect on them, which they were being forced to deal with, one way or another. Later, some of them did join me and became friends.

Under surveillance again

One young immigrant, a graduate of Seoul National University, told me that before his departure the KCIA had given orientation to those leaving for

Canada. They were advised not to go to the Korean United Church in Toronto because its minister was a communist. The young man laughed. As soon as he heard this, he said, he decided to join our congregation.

I have no way of knowing how many others kept their distance.

One day, a stranger came to see me. As he sank into the old couch which graces my office, he looked around at the overflowing bookshelves, the boxes of pamphlets and papers stacked here and there on the floor, the clutter on my desk. He seemed somewhat surprised at the cramped quarters of my office, especially the high round window with its cracked glass, the plastic storm screen, and the pigeons making contented noises just outside.

"I know you very well," the stranger finally announced. "Even before I came to Canada, I read all of your articles. I even listened to your radio programs."

"In Korea?" I asked in surprise.

The man smiled. "On tapes, of course. You are a famous man, didn't you know that?"

I realized then that this man must have been a KCIA agent. Someone in Toronto had taped our programs and sent them to Seoul.

He told me he had also read most of my father-in-law's books and articles, that he admired the clarity of his writing. "I'll be honest with you," he professed. "I have been sent by my government to confirm reports of your activities that have been sent monthly to Seoul by our embassy in Ottawa. A colleague there seems to be convinced that you are communists employed by the North Korean government. Frankly, I have watched you for several months now. I've observed your activities and listened to your talks and sermons, and I personally find no evidence of communism in any of it."

It was just a friendly call, he told me. He wanted me to know he gave me a clean bill of health.

I must admit I was taken aback. I had no idea that the Korean government was wasting so much effort on my behalf. Though I was pleased to hear that this agent say that he was prepared to clear my name, I soon realized he had ulterior motives. He wanted to talk with me, to persuade me that I had misunderstood the conduct of the Korean government.

From time to time, my father-in-law received telephone calls from his son and other daughter in Seoul. They had been pressured by the KCIA to beg him to stop his anti-government activities, for their sake. This was a terrible hardship for the old man. Graciously and tenderly, he comforted them. But also told them that precisely for their sake, he could not stop.

More and more Korean friends involved in human rights work told me their own stories of inquiries, warnings, bribes and blackmail by the KCIA here in Canada. Finally I approached the Foreign Affairs Department of the Canadian government in Ottawa. They listened politely but told me that without concrete evidence, they could do nothing. The KCIA knew very well how to create such subtle pressures that they could never be charged with anything. I wondered how seriously I was being taken; Canada was, at the time, rapidly increasing trade and commerce with the offending regime.

Church leaders imprisoned

One night I was wakened by a telephone call from overseas. My alarm clock said 2:15 a.m. Calls at that time almost always meant bad news. The voice at the other end was speaking from Tokyo. As he began his account, I fumbled for a pen and began to scribble on the pad I kept next to my telephone.

On March 1, 1976, some of the most prominent Korean church and opposition leaders had met at the Roman Catholic Cathedral in Seoul, to issue their most comprehensive statement to date about the national situation. The KCIA had discovered the plan. While the group was meeting, the police attacked the Cathedral and arrested all the signatories. Among those taken were my long-time friends, the brothers Moon Ik-Hwan and Moon Dong-Hwan, the Rev. Suh Nam-Dong, as well as presidential candidate Kim Dae-Jung and several Roman Catholic priests. The voice from Tokyo said the situation was critical—the detainees were undergoing torture and immediate international action was required.

I immediately informed other friends in the network. Reports began to circulate among churches, the media and in government circles.

As the arrest of these leaders came to light, public outrage developed internationally. The World Council of Churches, Amnesty International, and the United Nations Commission on Human Rights all voiced their concern. More significantly, they began to monitor more carefully the situation in Korea. More reports of atrocities in Korea began to appear in the media.

I reported the situation to the executives of both the Division of World

Outreach and the General Council of my church. The United Church decided to send its moderator to Korea to speak to government representatives. The moderator had a conflict of schedules, however, and could not go.

Somebody suggested that I should go instead. There were some chuckles. I suppose some members felt that it would be ironic for me to go, since I was a Korean, and already perceived to be a trouble-maker.

But the person making the proposal insisted that the United Church should make clear that Canadians of *any* background can legitimately represent the church as a whole. That settled it.

The only question was whether I would accept the risk of going. I felt that I could not refuse. If I could bring comfort to the prisoners and their families, and could show the solidarity of the Canadian church with churches in Korea, it would be worth whatever personal risk I might be exposed to.

I visited Seoul for ten days. The PROK asked me to deliver meditations during their five-day General Assembly. KCIA agents took notes from the balcony of the church. They followed me everywhere. A Canadian missionary stationed in Seoul became my unofficial "body guard." We knew that the government had no wish to create any unpleasant incidents involving Canadian citizens.

My request to visit the prisoners was refused. But despite KCIA efforts to keep me away from them, I did spend four hours with the wives of the prisoners. I was impressed and moved by their courage. Instead of sad faces betraying fear and despair, these women were so convinced of victory that they joked and laughed about their confrontations with KCIA agents.

"Don't feel sorry for us," they told me. "We know that our struggle is just. The suffering our husbands are going through is rewarded by the appreciation of the Korean people. The Gospel assures us that those who hunger and thirst for righteousness will be satisfied. Feel sorry instead for those agents following you around, because they are despised by the people, and they will ultimately be brought to justice."

The government's Minister of Culture and Information, who also dealt with church affairs, asked to see me. We met for two hours. He tried to explain the government's difficulties by saying that a firm hand was necessary to maintain South Korea's defenses against a North Korean invasion. I told them that his reasoning was not accepted by churches in Canada and elsewhere. The best way to keep South Korea strong was by demonstrating that it was a land where freedom, justice and peace prevailed.

He told me that his government suspected that the churches I represented had a left-wing orientation. They had read books about liberation theology, he told me. In their minds, "liberation theology" was thinly disguised communism, originating in the Soviet Union. We began to debate theology, but I quickly saw that he had no interest in open dialogue.

The US connection

After I returned to Canada, our network organized a conference in New York. Roughly 100 participants attended, including numerous mainline church leaders and representatives of international organizations like the World Council of Churches. A number of delegations were constituted to visit political leaders in the USA, Canada, West Germany and Sweden, to express the churches' concern about the violations of human rights and the arrest of religious leaders in Korea.

The North American Coalition for Democracy in Korea was founded, with Peggy Billings as chair and myself as vice-chair. Our worldwide network gained expertise and grew in numbers. We began to receive funding from some church agencies and from the World Council of Churches.

We met at least once a year, in different locations around the world. For the security of those members who attended from inside Korea, we observed strict confidentiality about these meetings. At that time, travel outside Korea was severely restricted. To permit our partners inside to obtain passports, trusted church leaders in the countries where we met issued invitations for legitimate but innocuous-sounding church events.

I had difficulties justifying these travels to my congregation. Because I was under constant surveillance, I could not announce my travel plans in advance. At one session meeting, therefore, I asked the church to trust me, and to allow me to absent myself occasionally without having to tell them where I was going or for what reason. They gave me that trust. It was an act I have deeply appreciated from my congregation.

Often I traveled to Washington. In the beginning, I naïvely thought that the USA, which prides itself as being the guarantor of freedom and democracy in the whole world, would be sympathetic. We had numerous meetings at the State Department and the Pentagon. But instead of being welcomed as partners sharing a common goal, we were treated at best like pathetic and somewhat ignorant idealists. "Can we expect a country as backward as Korea to be ready for democracy?" we were asked. "Until the confrontation between North and South is resolved, Korea is not ready for democracy."

Every time, I came away from those meetings seething with anger. I felt humiliated and insulted. I kept asking myself what Koreans had done to deserve this treatment. Koreans had not caused the Second World War, yet unlike West Germany and Japan, they were kept under dictatorship. Koreans did not divide their country, yet while East and West Germans can write, telephone, and even visit their relatives on the other side of the dividing line, Koreans are kept hermetically sealed from each other.

Thank God, some of the major American churches, and the National Council of Churches of Christ in the USA did heed the cries of Koreans.

The Kwangju massacre

When Park Chung-Hee was assassinated by the head of his own KCIA on October 26, 1979, we expected democracy to be restored. But on December 12, 1979, General Chun Doo-Hwan usurped power, with the help of troops led by General Roh Tae-Woo, the current president of Korea.

On May 17, 1980, Chun Doo-Hwan re-introduced martial law and arrested Kim Dae-Jung, the man most likely to have won a presidential election. Thousands of people flooded the streets in protest. The largest protests were in the city of Kwangju, in the home province of Kim Dae-Jung. Kwangju citizens held off police and troops for almost ten days, demanding a democratic constitution.

On May 27, the armed forces moved into Kwangju to suppress the uprising. Over 2,000 people were ruthlessly massacred. The assault was commanded by five generals, including current President Roh Tae Woo. Because Korean troops came under US command, Kwangju residents insist that US generals must have approved the use of these troops to quell the uprising; the US denies any involvement.

Inside Korea, people started seriously re-thinking the US role. For the first time, anti-American slogans appeared. By contrast, during a previous student demonstration while I still lived in Korea, the students had taken time out to place a wreath at the statue of General Douglas MacArthur.

Contacts with the North

In our international organization, some had insisted from the first that human rights and democracy took precedence over everything else. Others were pessimistic about achieving any real changes in the South as long as a threat from the North could be used as an excuse to continue the dictatorship in the South. These persons argued that we should first try to re-unify the country, and then fight for democracy in both parts.

The advocates of this second position began to make overtures to North Korea, opening contacts and also making visits there. Some of them found and visited long-lost relatives. They came back with photographs and moving stories of family reunions. Excitement swept through the movement, especially among those of us who longed to see parents and relatives from whom we had been so long separated.

North Korea, of course, saw this as an opportunity to improve its international image. It invited a number of overseas Koreans to visit, on the chance that they too might find their relatives. Both my father-in-law and I received invitations.

I was so excited, I could not sleep for several nights. But though I yearned to accept, I knew that my decision could have grave consequences for others. I had to make sure that my own desires did not jeopardize other separated families, and that there would be no repercussions on my friends in South Korea. I circulated about 35 letters asking for advice. Except for one positive response, every reply urged us not to accept an invitation to North Korea at this time. If we did, they said, the government would surely claim our visits as proof that the democratic movement in South Korea was linked with North Korean communists. The time was not ripe for an opening towards the North. I must continue to be patient.

These replies came as a terrible blow. I complained bitterly to God. For weeks I had clung to a hope that I might see my parents again, or if they were no longer alive, at least my sisters and brothers. It seemed unfair. I myself had no family at all in the South, but I had to discipline myself, in the distant hope that somehow, justice and peace for the whole Korean peninsula would be served. But did I really have such a hope?

Because we refused their invitation, North Korea began to consider my father-in-law and me as hostile. We joked, grimly, about being blacklisted by the South as communists and by the North as anti-communists.

Linking the homeless

I began to doubt that we would ever win. But how could I give up? If I admitted defeat, I would have to concede victory to evil. That I was not prepared to do. I took comfort from the life of Christ who knew much greater loneliness and pain, yet endured and showed by his example that what seems like failure in human terms may be God's victory. I sensed the invisible power of the Holy Spirit sustaining me, giving me strength to continue one step at a time, stubbornly plodding along, even if our cause was making only slow progress.

From time to time I have reflected, with amusement, that I have reason to thank Park Chung-Hee and Chun Doo-Hwan. Through my involvement in the struggle against their oppression, I learned things I never would have learned, made friends I never would have met, and experienced life at a much more profound level.

In the last two years, some battles have been won. The re-unification of Korea has risen to a higher place on the world's agenda. The World Council of Churches has opened lines of communication with Christians in North Korea. Christians from North and South Korea have had two historic encounters. In the fall of 1988, the first Canadian church delegation visited North Korean Christians and brought back videotapes of the first two churches to be built in the North since the Korean war.

In 1986 I had the opportunity of re-visiting Manchuria, on the invitation of the Chinese government. Millions of Koreans still live in that part of China. Unfortunately, Chinese authorities could not trace my family. I visited the town where we last lived, but no one there knew of them. This confirms my suspicion that they moved to North Korea soon after I left.

The trip made me newly aware of the great number of Koreans living outside of Korea. Estimates run as high as six million. There are Koreans in China, Japan, the USA, Canada, Western Europe, the USSR, Latin America Australia, and even in a small number of communities in Africa.

I have long felt that someone should create a network to link these people, many of whom live in desperate isolation. Sometimes I dare to believe that the tragedy of Korea might be turned into a benefit for human-kind. Like the world as a whole, our people have long been divided. We have become scattered across the globe in a diaspora, living under every kind of social and ideological system. If we could build community across all the barriers that separate us, then perhaps we might teach the world to do the same.

I don't think I have any worry about being bored after my retirement.

Uniquely Canadian

The Korean community in Toronto has done well in the past 20 years. We have maintained our Korean identity, while becoming more Canadian.

As it happens, being Canadian is a subject I endlessly emphasize to my flock. I tell them repeatedly: "You live here, you work here, you buy a house here, you build up a business here. Your children live here; you will probably die here. There is no turning back. You have to take seriously that Canada is your adopted country. You have to put down roots here. You have to consider yourselves Canadian."

I often remind them of Japanese immigrants before World War II. Many thought they would come to Canada, make some money, and then return. Some did return, but they found that they were no longer attuned to Japanese society. They felt more like strangers in Japan than in Canada.

At first, Korean immigrants were unhappy to hear me talk like this. Some walked out in the middle of my lecture. I don't blame them. It is not easy to adjust to this society when you have not mastered English, when you are not used to the culture that surrounds you, and when your physical features always identify you as a foreigner.

The recent public debate in Canada about racism, as painful as it may be, will do this country a lot of good. I have found most European-origin Canadians to be wonderfully open people. But racism does exist.

The internment of the Japanese during the war was certainly an example of institutional racism. I am glad that the Canadian government has finally acknowledged this injustice.

Racial tensions occasionally surfaced at Steveston in Vancouver. One day our youngest daughter Joy came home from school, sobbing. One of the boys had followed her all the way home, calling her racist names and spitting on her face.

I was extremely angry. I took only enough time to put on my clerical outfit, and then went with my daughter to the boy's house. The parents scolded the boy and made him apologize. It has always made me sad to see how quickly young children pick up racist attitudes.

Sometimes racism comes out more overtly. When I was in training as a counselor in hospitals, some people either refused to speak to me because of my race, or used foul language in my presence.

A country open to all

Canadians often ask why Koreans came to Canada. I suppose they want to hear about the plight of Korea, the North-South conflict, the economic situation, the unrest. But I prefer to make a point about what it means to be "Canadian."

I tell them of a beautiful song I learned in Canada. Its words say "This land is your land, this land is my land... This land was made for you and me." They usually laugh, and comment that they have all sung that song.

So I ask them, "To whom do you refer when you sing 'you'?" They usually stare blankly at me. So I answer for them: "I think you are referring to us Koreans."

This elicits polite laughter. But it's not a joke at all. If Canada is a country open to European immigration, then it must be open to every other type of immigration as well. If not, we had better leave it to the Native people from whom it was taken in the first place.

Getting involved

I stress to my own people that we must not shut ourselves up in our own ethnic ghettos. Several times a year, I organize weekend retreats. A young third-generation Canadian of Japanese descent told us his frustration at always being asked when he had come to Canada, and why his English was so good. A fourth-generation Jewish Canadian told us how his ancestors looked English, but had to change their names in order to get jobs. He suggested that we have to show Anglo-Saxon Canadians that we can compete as equals with them. He cited statistics on how many Jews are doctors, lawyers, etc.

"But not everyone can become a professional," I countered. "We also need carpenters and plumbers and non-skilled laborers. And they need to be treated equally well."

The "achievement syndrome" that affects many immigrant families can have a devastating effect on those young people who do not have the necessary abilities.

Nonetheless, I have always felt strongly that those who have ability should be willing to take leadership in public life, within the church or outside. Having learned the hard way that every segment of human life has something to do with politics, I have badgered Koreans to get involved politically. Most agreed in principle, but had little idea how to make any impact. Our numbers, comparatively, are still very small. They did not wish to seem "pushy," or ask for special consideration. This is a common fear of "outsiders," who do not wish to draw attention to themselves.

The year I was elected president of the Toronto Conference of The United Church of Canada, the government of the province of Ontario changed. By custom, religious leaders are invited to participate in the swearing-in of the new cabinet at the Ontario Legislature. It must have looked funny to see a tall Anglo-Saxon premier and his cabinet being blessed by a small Asian with a white beard! All the same, I hoped it would make a statement, to these political leaders and the press, about this marvelously inclusive country of ours.

Some time later, I received a letter from Premier David Peterson inviting me to come and talk about the Korean community. During our talk, I raised the question of Korean membership in the Liberal Party. Premier Peterson pointed out that anyone, of any origin, may freely join the party in a local riding. I explained to him the difficulty that Koreans, or members of any linguistic or visible minority, have in making themselves heard when they have to fragment themselves geographically among various ridings. Would it not be possible for Koreans to organize themselves and join as a group?

Peterson said his party's by-laws made this impossible. I asked him, "Aren't you guys the ones who create and change laws and regulations?" He laughed and said he would look into the matter.

Since then, the rules *have* changed. A number of Koreans became the first ethnic branch of any political party in Canada. After the Koreans organized, other ethnic groups have done the same. There are now Chinese, Philippine, Pakistani and Indian organizations within Canadian parties, and the list is growing. The ethnic groups in the Liberal Party have even formed an umbrella organization to discuss common problems and dealt with them in a politically effective way.

Our young people have become more active in Canadian public life. The numbers are still small. But the potential for playing an important role for the future of Canada does not depend on numbers.

Cleaning up our own act

At the same time, we who are immigrants must be vigilant and self-critical. We can be just as narrow-minded and thoughtless as those we criticize. I have had to recognize this truth in my own life.

Once, in Vancouver, I ran into a classic example of immigrant prejudices. A Japanese-Canadian came to my office with his German-Canadian girlfriend. They asked me to marry them, right there, on the spot.

I felt that there was something wrong. After we talked for a while, the truth emerged. Their parents, on both sides, opposed this match. I suggested that they postpone the wedding ceremony until I had a chance to talk to the parents. The couple looked skeptical, but wished me luck.

I went to the Japanese family first, expecting to be able to persuade them more easily because I could speak their language. The young man's parents told me that they were not against their son's marrying a foreign woman. What bothered them was that she was German. The Germans had been so brutal in World War II, they said, that they wanted nothing more to do with them.

I pointed out to them that the Japanese had a reputation of being just as brutal. But I failed to convince them.

Then I visited the German parents. To my amazement, I heard exactly the same story. The Japanese, they said, had been such a brutal people, they would be ashamed to have their daughter married to one. Again, I pointed out that Japan and Germany had been allies; both shared an infamous reputation. They refused to give in.

About two weeks passed. The young couple told me both sets of parents had at least agreed to attend the wedding. Two more weeks passed. The young couple came back again, extremely happy. The four parents had met, and had decided to invite *all* their families and friends to the wedding.

In our own family, too

I didn't realize I would face the same situation in my own life, not just once, but three times.

My wife and I, like most parents, worried about our three daughters— the oldest, Irene (Lee Chung-Wha), then Grace (Lee Chung-Sun), and our youngest, Joy (Lee Chung-Hee)—hoping that they might find happiness in their lives, fulfillment in their careers, and suitable mates to marry. We tried to raise them to have respect for themselves and for others, regardless of background, culture, or religion.

Of course, we always assumed that they would eventually marry young men of Korean origin. But when they began to take an interest in boys, we realized that they did not necessarily share our assumption. To clarify things before any serious relationships developed, we called the family together for an earnest conversation.

We told them that marriage is a serious proposition; that the divorce rate in society is rising constantly; that we wanted them to be truly happy in their married lives; that they should consider very carefully their choice of mates; and that, of course, we expected them to marry our own kind of people.

Our daughters listened attentively. Then they told us, unanimously, that they understood our concern, that they appreciated our worry, and that they would consider our suggestions. On the other hand, they added, they could give no guarantee they would follow our advice.

Before long, Grace informed us that she was serious about Douglas Alexander Scott, her boyfriend for five years. We tried to dissuade her. But we really had no valid arguments. Doug was a good boy, whom everybody liked. His parents, a father of Scottish and a mother of Irish descent, were wonderful people and accepted our daughter wholeheartedly.

Still, my wife and I had a lot of hesitations.

One evening, Grace came to my study. She reminded me that once in Steveston I had preached a sermon about race relations. I had emphasized that no matter what our race, or our culture, or our language, we are all the children of the same God. She had been impressed by that sermon, she said.

It had given her courage to persevere in school. "When you were preaching, you were always so clear, so strong, so positive about racial relationships. But when your own daughter is going out with a fellow of another race, you are so stubborn. How come?" she wanted to know.

I didn't remembered that particular sermon, but I had preached similar things many times. My daughter had given me a lot of cause for self-reflection.

Sometime after that encounter, Doug came to see me about marrying Grace. I knew we had reached the point of no return. Everyone in the house was on edge that day, not knowing how I would react.

Doug and Grace arrived, visibly nervous, but also resolute. Before the assembled family, Doug said they had been going out now for five years. They had discussed this for a long time, and were sure that they were meant for each other. They had made up their minds to be married. They asked for my approval.

There was a pause. No one breathed.

I told them that my wife Kim Shin-Jah and I had discussed and prayed about their wish for some time. We had concluded that if they truly loved each other and were determined to marry, we would bless their marriage.

Another pause as my words sank in. Then the tension began to drain from the faces of the young man and the three sisters. Actually, I was rather relieved myself. The ice had been broken, and as I looked into the beaming, grateful eyes of my daughter, the ice in my heart began to melt as well.

They told me that their wedding would be very small, with only close friends and relatives invited. I suspected I might be the reason for this decision. I was right. Grace said that, considering my position in the Korean community, I might not be proud of this marriage. I replied, "No, my child, this is going to be a big wedding. Once I have blessed your marriage, you may be sure that I am really and truly proud of you."

Some 500 guests came to that wedding, including many prominent people in the Korean community. After the service, several parishioners confided that they were in exactly the same situation. I suddenly realized that numerous sons and daughters of Koreans were living through the same painful tension with their parents. The open pride that I showed in my daughter's wedding had been a source of encouragement for many in my community.

I thanked God for teaching me what I had so often tried to teach others. And I humbly asked God to forgive my own narrow-mindedness.

Our oldest daughter, Irene, decided to seek a Korean husband—perhaps to make her parents happy. She traveled to Korea. My wife's relatives introduced her to a number of young men. Unfortunately, things did not work out. It was a painful experience, and I felt some guilt for having emphasized too greatly my wish to see our daughters marry a Korean.

Fortunately, Irene decided to continue her education and went to Windsor, Ontario, to study for a Master's degree in Social Work. There she met Peter Dirks, another Social Work graduate student. Peter came from an Estonian background: his grandfather, I was told, had been a Mennonite minister. Peter and Irene were married about three years later.

Our youngest daughter, Joy, married John Cappelleti, a boy of Italian extraction, raised in a Roman Catholic home. They had met in high school and gone to the University of Toronto together. They had known each other about ten years before they were married.

So ultimately, none of our three daughters married Koreans. But I feel no disappointment; I can only thank God that all three have found such happiness in their lives.

Grace was the first to gift us with grandchildren. After completing her education degree at York University, and then working for an accounting firm, she began to raise her own family. It was a strange but wonderful experience when our first grandson, Michael Lee Scott, was born, followed

Multicultural grandchildren: Michelle, Michael, and Andrea

by a granddaughter, Michelle Elizabeth Scott. Grace's husband Douglas, a community college graduate, is an electronics technologist for a computer company in Toronto.

Irene works as a Social Worker for the Board of Education in Chatham, Ontario. Her husband Peter works for the Ontario Government. Last year God blessed them with a daughter, Andrea Marie Kim Dirks, adding a sweet new granddaughter to my rapidly expanding extended family.

Joy is currently a Grade One school teacher, in Richmond Hill, Ontario. She hopes soon to return to her specialty, working with handicapped and disabled children. Her husband John, a political science graduate, works for the Roman Catholic School Board as Public Relations Officer.

It is a pleasure to behold how these three families have become such close friends. And it is a wonderful new experience to be grandparents. Sometimes I have an impression of being a patriarch to a growing multicultural family. Perhaps we are more genuinely Canadian than most families in Canada in that respect, more representative of the range of cultures that make up this country.

Though I had preached diversity for so long, I had little idea that it could be so much fun. I had worried about how my wife would get along with non-Korean sons-in-law and English-speaking grandchildren. She has always been shy, and struggles valiantly with the complexities of the English language. But in fact, she is doing much better than I am. If I say anything that strikes her as too critical of "our boys," she immediately corrects me. She is proud of them, and lets me know it.

Sometimes I can hardly believe how fortunate I have been. Neither my grandfather nor my father were ever able to have their entire families so near to them. Neither of them could ever look to the future with so much hope and confidence.

Overcoming bigotry

Having experienced in my own family the joys of racial harmony, I have become even more impatient with racial bigotry. From time to time I overhear Koreans casually using derogatory terms to refer to black people, for example. More than once I have scolded people for their careless use of words. I tell them that even more than others, we Koreans should be sensitive, remembering our own historical experience of discrimination and oppression.

During our various human rights struggles, I have had the privilege of getting to know the situation of blacks in North America, who were brought as slaves to this continent. I have also come to know the reality of native people in Canada. We later immigrants must be careful not to add to the injustice of the earlier settlers of this continent. We share in the gains resulting from evils committed in earlier periods of history. We should support wholeheartedly efforts to alleviate the effects of those wrongs. That is why, although I am a new Canadian, I felt no hesitation about participating in The United Church of Canada's apology to Native People.

My experience with the human rights movement has made clear to me that theology does not come out of the sky, as something ideal or theoretical. It has to come from the life and death experience, from the sufferings and struggles, of the community of faith. It has to respond to what God teaches us through human experience. Theology must therefore always be open-ended, receptive to God's teaching in the present historical circumstances.

I have read the Bible now for almost 40 years. Yet I am constantly enlightened with new insights. Stories which I had often read before suddenly contain totally new perspectives. Struggling with the question of racism, for example, I re-read the book of Esther in the Old Testament. Before, I had always seen Esther and her people's suffering merely as the result of their loyalty to God. But now I also saw them as victims of racism. If we look at scriptures with a closed mind, as though we already had all the wisdom necessary to understand God's word, we shut out the Holy Spirit—no matter how right we might think we are.

In The United Church of Canada, we have a unique opportunity to develop new models of theological diversity, just as in Canada we have a unique opportunity to develop new models of living together without discrimination of language, culture, race, sex or class. If we can successfully create harmony and unity in this country, with its diversity of peoples, we will make a unique contribution to the rest of the world. And if our church could generate a theology rooted in the experience of all our people, then we in turn could make a unique contribution to this country.

A symbol of an open-minded church

I hope that my election as moderator of The United Church of Canada symbolizes that the church is taking seriously its diverse cultural and ethnic composition. I am sure that this election will encourage many ethnic members to participate more fully in the life of the church. I hope that it will also signal that those of us from cultures not represented by Canada's two official languages, English and French, are ready to take responsibility in Canadian society.

For this reason, and for no other, I agreed to let my name stand for election. To tell the truth, I dreaded making that decision. One character trait has changed little over the course of the years—I always have some inner resistance to taking on positions of responsibility. Mine is hardly the story of a driving, ambitious man. On the contrary. Whenever I dare to look deep inside of me, I still see the frightened boy who escaped to South Korea, the insecure young man who hesitated so long before getting married, the theology graduate who had to be pushed into ordination.

Sang-Chul and Shin-Jah Lee, at the time of his election as moderator, at the United Church's General Council in Victoria, B.C., in August 1988.

Then how do I get myself into these positions? I will resist the temptation to blame God for everything that happened to me during my life! But just as with my baptism, all along the way I have been pressed, urged, nagged, cajoled or simply ordered from one responsibility to the next. Whether it was superiors, colleagues, friends or relatives doesn't really matter. Whether I knew what I was getting into or not doesn't really matter. God knew. And that simple assurance has kept me going all these years.

Being a token is a ministry too

When I look back over my 25 years in Canada, I can list over 25 positions of leadership I have held, in the United Church and in the Korean community—not counting my pastorates or being moderator! I remember how unpleasant some of these meetings were, how often I promised myself never again to return, how often I was fed up with the bureaucracy, the meaningless arguments, the hypocrisy, the closed-mindedness, the racism, the lack of progress.

Yet always some voice inside kept insisting that somebody has to present your point of view, your experience, because you are not merely an individual. You represent a community.

I often felt I was being treated like a stranger. As the only non-white in many meetings, I had the impression of being a token. I could sit there, I would be treated politely, I would be listened to.

But was I heard?

Perhaps I should have engaged in battle more often, expressed my anger and frustration more often, demanded more attention. Or perhaps I should have stuck to doing what I love the most—being a pastor, a counsellor on a one-to-one basis, caring for people who are neglected by the mainstream, who cannot cope alone in a hostile world.

But something within me has never allowed me to escape so easily. As God has shown me throughout my life, the easy escape into the personal while neglecting the institutional is an abdication of full responsibility. We need both—we cannot neglect the institutional anymore than we can neglect the personal. They are interconnected, interlinked. To serve the individuals in my community, I had to care also for their integration into society as a whole, into the church as one community of believers.

Being a token is also a calling. Perhaps I will not accomplish much in the two short years that a moderator holds office in The United Church of Canada. But I am there as a sign, a symbol. And once in a while, when the tensions mount, when the arguments become overwhelming, one who has stood outside the polemics might lead the way towards peace.

The human rights movement has seen many examples of intense conflict among colleagues. Occasionally, I have played a peace-making role. I am not easily swayed by posturing. I guess that comes from learning early in life that power and wealth and status do not in themselves deserve respect. Perhaps reconciliation depends on distinguishing between conflicts that should be taken seriously and conflicts that should be laughed at.

To face conflicts in the church or in the world, we first have to face the conflicts within ourselves. If I am a peace-maker, it is perhaps because I have had to deal with so many conflicts inside myself.

A model for the world

I don't know why God chose this particular moment for me to become moderator of the United Church of Canada. During the first months after my election, everywhere I went I was badgered by the press about the conflict in our church over the right of homosexual persons to be considered for ordination. I claim no expertise on the subject of sexual orientation. I am disturbed, however, that dogmatic judgements rather than love and compassion dominate much of our discussions.

The present conflict is only the latest of many that our church has faced. Those who have already decided to leave the church say this is "the last straw." I condemn no one for leaving our church. I wish they would stay, to struggle and grow with us, because The United Church of Canada is for those who can live with conflict. Conflict is written into the very constitution of our church. In their wisdom, the founders of The United Church of Canada refused to accept one theological position over another. Not because, as some have charged, they wished to "water down" theology, but because they believed that in diversity lies the grace of God. In this faith, many challenges have been faced in the past. And if we continue to face challenges instead of running from them, our church will remain the dynamic force it has so often been.

I find it ironic that during my moderatorship so many people seem to have decided that their only recourse is to leave the church. For the first person to mention the possibility of my becoming moderator was himself driven out of the church he had faithfully served throughout his life. But Kim Chai-Choon, my father-in-law, never threatened to leave in order to put pressure on his church, as so many are doing today. He believed that the Holy Spirit is much greater than our limited human minds can comprehend. He believed that the church has a place for all, sinners and saints, conservatives and liberals. He believed that no one has a monopoly on truth.

I think we must seek the truth all our lives long, as he himself did. His theology evolved and changed and grew throughout his life. He taught me the humility of always being open for new insights in the faith, and never believing I had fully grasped the wisdom of God. Kim Chai-Choon's church could not accept such theological maturity, and suspended him.

It was this man who first proposed, many years ago, that I let my name stand as candidate for the United Church's moderatorship. I remember laughing. "Don't ask for the impossible," I told him. Only now have I realized that he believed even more strongly in the inclusive character of The United Church of Canada than I did.

In 1983 he moved back to Korea, after spending almost ten years in Canada. The last time I saw him was in the fall of 1984. He insisted that I come to see him after a World Council of Churches' conference in Japan on the re-unification of Korea. Surprisingly, I received an entry visa for Korea, though once again the KCIA followed me everywhere.

"Do something about that moderatorship!" he ordered me when I met him. I laughed again, but he was serious.

He died in the Spring of 1986. I mourned him terribly. He had taken the place of my father, guiding me, encouraging me, instilling faith in myself and strengthening my faith in God.

I have found a powerful image of the church in the experience of Pentecost. At Pentecost, the Holy Spirit blew like a strong wind and appeared like tongues of fire. When our faith is tossed and turned in the wind and conflicts erupt like fire, then we should thank God. These are the signs of the movement of the Holy Spirit, shaking us up, filling us with passion, and strengthening and comforting us in our struggles.

The church founded by that upper room experience in Jerusalem was not a homogeneous, uniform community. They were a bit like Canada and our church—multiracial, multicultural and multilingual. Read the response to the coming of the Spirit: "We are from Parthia, Media and Elam; from Mesopotamia, Judea and Cappadocia; from Pontus and Asia; from Phrygia and Pamphylia; from Egypt and the regions of Libya near Cyrene. Some of us are from Rome, both Jews and Gentiles converted to Judaism, and some of us are from Crete and Arabia—yet all of us hear [this message] in our own languages!" (Acts 2:9-11)

This confused and colorful conglomeration was not simply a coincidence. God intended the original form of the Christian congregation to be a diverse and multicultural community. Revelation 7:9 reinforces this insight when it describes the completed Kingdom of God: "I looked, and there was an enormous crowd... from every race, tribe, nation and language...."

The vision of the Kingdom of God is inclusive, not exclusive. Whatever the church can do to expand and complete its own inclusiveness moves us in the direction of the Kingdom of God.

I am thankful that God allowed me to become a participant in this inclusiveness. The beginning of my life showed me the tragedy of rejection, of separation, of being a stranger in a strange land. I have spent my life as a wanderer, a refugee five times over. All the more I have come to value the immeasurable grace of God in filling my later life with so much love, so much participation, so much community.

My prayer is that my becoming Moderator of The United Church of Canada may be seen as a symbol, however insignificant, of God's all-inclusive purpose, a small glimmer of hope that our church, our country and our world can succeed in living in unity, in peace and with justice for all according to God's will and wisdom.

Canada has a challenge and an opportunity, as a multi-cultural society already, to demonstrate the possibilities of such a society. I believe that this is the century when our whole world is trying to learn how to live together. And as the international tensions of the cold war change, global solidarity becomes a real possibility. The United Church of Canada, which started by bringing together into one body three distinct and different denominations, has begun that process. As a church, as a nation, as a world, we need spiritual leaders who can embrace these possibilities, and encourage us all to move further along that path.